THE ASSAULT ON JUDAISM

THE EXISTENTIAL THREAT IS COMING FROM THE WEST

GOL KALEV

To Tamar

TABLE OF CONTENTS

INTRODUCTION

IT IS HAPPENING

On October 7, 2023, Hamas stunned the world with a brutal invasion of Israel, murdering, raping, beheading, and burning alive hundreds of Israelis, as well as kidnapping about 250 hostages and taking them into Gaza. This was the worst attack on the Jewish nation since the Holocaust.

Speaking about it seven months later at Israel's Holocaust Remembrance Day ceremony, Israel's Prime Minister Benjamin Netanyahu clarified, "The horrific terrorist attack of October 7th was not a Holocaust. Not because they lacked the intent of genocide, but because they lacked the ability to carry it out."

Indeed, Hamas does not have the capabilities to eradicate the Jewish nation—but the West does. These capabilities are housed in bodies such as the International Criminal Court which could issue arrest warrants for Israeli Jews en masse, as well as in governments that could sanction Israeli Jews, confiscate Israeli companies' assets, and deliver a devastating blow to the Israeli economy. It is supported by the capabilities of the Western media that could incite the world against the Jews, delegitimize contemporary Jewish life, instill a global consciousness that the world order is disrupted by Jews, and usher Jews themselves into a state of demoralization and attrition.

Those capabilities, which had been dormant and merely theoretical, were activated on October 7th and today Judaism is facing its greatest existential threat in two thousand years—since the Romans deported the Jews from Judea.

Indeed, days after Hamas attacked from Gaza, a secondary assault on the Jewish nation was launched from the West. At its core was an aggressive incitement against Israel in mainstream Western media, at times reporting Hamas talking points verbatim as facts, and using creative wording of headlines that amounted to anti-Jewish propaganda reminiscent of 1940s Germany.

This was followed a few days later by the UN turning the atrocious Hamas attack around and providing justification. "October 7th did not happen in a vacuum," UN Secretary-General Antonio Guterres declared on October 24th. Soon world leaders joined in, echoing the same accusations leveled against Jews for centuries, including insinuations that the Jewish state is killing women, children, and babies (Canadian Prime Minister Justin Trudeau), dehumanizing others and even poisoning our common well (U.S. Secretary of State Blinken). By March 14th, Senator Chuck Schumer took the daring step of parroting the bile heard throughout the centuries—from Persia during the Book of Esther, through Europe during the Holocaust: Indeed, the Jewish state is "a pariah opposed by the rest of the world."

By April, Jewish students in universities throughout the United States were being harassed, in some cases blocked by protesters from going to classes. Jews across the United States and Europe swiftly removed the Star of David necklaces from their necks and Mezuzahs from their doors. A debate in the Jewish community and the general public erupted: Is what we are witnessing antisemitism or merely criticism of Israel? Are we in 1930s Germany? Is left-wing antisemitism ("Jews dehumanize Palestinians") worse than right-wing antisemitism ("Jews will not replace us")?

These are the wrong questions. They merely distract us from internalizing the gloomy big picture: we are in the midst of a well-advanced effort to eradicate Judaism.

Every few centuries there is a large-scale assault on Judaism. Each time, it is conducted through mechanisms relevant to contemporary circumstances. Sometimes it is done through an attempt to destroy Judaism collectively as an idea, such as in Spain during the 15th century and Greece during the 2nd century BC. Sometimes it is done through an attempt to kill Jew by Jew, such as in Europe during the 20th century and during the crusades of the 12th century.

Today, Hamas, Iran, and its proxies are attempting to destroy Judaism Jew by Jew. They make no secret of their goal to kill all Jews, wherever they are. Indeed, Hamas succeeded in killing twelve hundred Jews in one day on October 7th, and Iran's missiles launched at Israel in April 2024 had the potential to kill thousands more in one hour. Yet, as Netanyahu suggested, they do not have the capabilities to eradicate Judaism. The existential threat to Judaism comes through the other path: eradication of Judaism collectively as an idea, and by mid-2024 that effort was well on its way.

Like previous large-scale assaults, the attack on Judaism is being channeled through the most relevant aspect of Judaism at the time. In our era, this aspect is Zionism, which has become the anchor of Judaism. Zionism is not the cause of the assault on the Jewish nation. It is the vehicle through which age-old opposition to Judaism is now being carried out.

As in previous assaults on Judaism, here too, the destruction mechanisms have been activated gradually. In February 2024, the U.S. stunned Israelis when it began sanctioning Israeli Jews—first targeting individuals in the fringe of society, then targeting organizations, and by April 2024 targeting the Israeli military! By early May, word had come out that the International Criminal Court was considering issuing arrest warrants against the Jewish state's leaders, military commanders, and even its soldiers. This would mean arrests of Israel's Jewish population, since Israeli citizens serve in reserve duty and left their families, businesses, and civilian life in October 2023 to fight for Israel's survival.

Indeed, on May 19th, the prosecutor of the International Criminal Court requested the arrest of Israeli Prime Minister Netanyahu and Defense Minister Yoav Gallant and laid the foundation for arrests of soldiers, who, the ICC stated, were part of collective crimes committed by the Israeli army: the deliberate starvation of civilian population and other alleged atrocities. "My Office will not hesitate to submit further applications for warrants of arrest," he proclaimed.

European countries, like France, who had participated in the last attempt to eradicate Judaism, jumped on board and stated that they would indeed arrest the Israeli prime minister if a warrant is issued—which some international law scholars view as a potential act of war against the Jewish state. Like a century prior, when arrest warrants were issued against the Jews, countries like France and Norway clarified: the law is the law, we will comply and arrest the Jews.

The threat escalated as word came that such arrest warrants would be issued without advance notice. This would ground Israelis in Israel, preventing Israeli Jews from running their businesses and robbing them of the "luxury" of attending meetings, participating in conferences, and going on vacations abroad. In parallel, an attempt to demoralize Israeli society was in its advanced stages.

Similar to previous assaults on Judaism, the assault is carried out not just by avid Israel-bashers but also by mainstream people who have acquiesced to the haters' pressure or believe they are doing the right thing, given decades of incitement and indoctrination. (In the 20th century, many Germans who murdered Jews claimed to do so not due to antisemitism but as an expression of their loyalty to Germany. They truly believed the Jews were the enemy.)

Israeli Jews are not the only ones threatened. Jews of the Diaspora account for about half of the world's Jewish population, 80 percent of whom reside in North America. The message broadcasted to them is that it is really not worth it to be Jewish. In many circles, Jews are beginning to feel guilty for an alleged genocide, starvation, and crimes against humanity that they had nothing to do with. A person of Jewish ancestry who has not thought of Judaism for decades has been drawn into his Judaism by a finger angrily pointed at him by his peers.

This has given rise to the idea that American Jews can carve themselves into "good Jews" in America, who are separate from the "bad Jews" in Israel. It's an understandable, yet historically ignorant idea. Many Jews in Germany in the 1930s, for example, believed that as loyal German citizens they were safe and that the assault was really against the Russian Jewish immigrants who "you see everywhere"—in the streets of Munich, in the cafes of Berlin, and in the workplace. Those "good German Jews" were proven wrong and so were Jews throughout history who tried to make this intra-Jewish distinction.

As in previous assaults on Judaism, trying to distance oneself from the aspect of Judaism being attacked is futile. A Jewish person can declare he is an anti-Zionist, attend pro-Palestinian demonstrations, and even express support for Hamas, and he will still be targeted. Indeed, Jews who disavowed any and all connection to Judaism were targeted in 15th century Spain and 20th century Europe. Such is the case today. The attack on Judaism in the 2020s affects all Jews, including those who bash Israel themselves.

For example, the *New York Times*, which has long been accused of being on the forefront of Israel-bashing and inciting against the Jewish state, is perceived to be owned by Jews. Therefore, on May 5, 2024, pro-Palestinian demonstrators blocked the entrance to the newspaper's Times Square headquarters chanting: "*New York Times*, you can't hide, we charge you with genocide."

Judaism is under assault from the West, and Jews cannot escape. Israeli public relations are futile since the Israel-bashing ideology is too entrenched in Western society by now and dogmatic minds cannot change.

"In every generation, someone rises up to eradicate us," the popular Jewish motto, turned song, goes. For Jews in 2023, this was a motto about faraway history—something we mention in the Passover Seder before we resume our normal, peaceful life. For Jews in 2024, within a few short months, this became a motto that describes their contemporary life.

Over the last decade, I discussed the brewing assault on Judaism in various forums, including in my book *Judaism 3.0: Judaism's Transformation to Zionism*, in my "Judaism 3.0" column in the *Jerusalem Post*, and in the Judaism 3.0 think tank. I have been arguing that Judaism is going through a historic transformation and Zionism is becoming its anchor. Increasingly, Jews and non-Jews relate to Judaism through the prism of Zionism and the Jewish state. Therefore it is no surprise that the modern-day attempt to eradicate Judaism is happening via an attack on Zionism. I argued that anti-Zionism, and more precisely Israel-bashing, is our era's attempt to eradicate Judaism. On September 13, 2023, we held a Judaism 3.0 think tank symposium in Jerusalem about the assault on Judaism now percolating in the West, describing the path to the destruction of Judaism through Israel-bashing and how a broad recognition that we are in Judaism 3.0 can counter that threat. Little did we know that this path would be triggered so soon.

The assault on Judaism needs to be treated through a paradigm shift—abandoning old conceptions and defending against it strategically as one would defend an existential military threat. This is what the last part of the book does.

As Judaism is facing a dual assault—a physical assault by Hamas, Iran, and its proxies, and an ideological assault coming from the West—it is heartwarming to receive so many messages of support from friends around the world—Muslims, Christians, and Jews—who state that they want to take part in the efforts to save Judaism.

To do that, we need to first understand the inner dynamics as well as the nuances of the assault and place it in its historical and strategic contexts.

BACKGROUND

CHAPTER 1

HISTORICAL ATTEMPTS TO ERADICATE JUDAISM

All the Jewish holidays have a common theme, according to the old joke, "They tried to kill us, we survived, let's eat."

Indeed, every few centuries there is a large-scale assault on Judaism. Each time, it is carried out through the most relevant aspect of Judaism of that time, using destruction mechanisms that are the most effective for that period and originating from the dominant entity of that era, which possesses the necessary destruction mechanisms.

In every episode, the attempt to eradicate Judaism has been carried out on a dual track: An ideological assault incites the public opinion against the Jews, while a physical assault is carried out to execute actual murders. Those two tracks, the ideological and physical, are often autonomous, but interdependent.

PERSIANS (PURIM)

In the 5th century BC, the dominant global power was Persia. The Biblical book of Esther describes its rule of 127 provinces from India to Africa. Persia was an adamantly pro-Jewish kingdom. Jews, who were exiled from Judea by the previous power, Babylonia, were scattered throughout the kingdom but seemed to prosper. Most notably, the Persian king Cyrus granted permission for Jews to return to their ancestral homeland and rebuild their Temple, which had been destroyed by the Babylonians.

Yet, not everybody in Persia was pro-Jewish. Haman, adviser to the king who succeeded Cyrus, launched an ideological campaign against the Jews, centered on the theme that the Jewish nation was a pariah that posed a great danger to global stability. He told the king, "There is one nation scattered and dispersed among the nations throughout the provinces of your kingdom, whose laws are unlike those of any other nation and who do not obey the laws of the King. It is not in the King's interest to tolerate them."

A mechanism was put in place to eradicate the Jews—a mechanism that was relevant to the time and, like all attempts to destroy Judaism, included an ideological and a physical component. The ideological component was a creative twist developed by Haman: not only are the Jews a pariah, opposed by the rest of the world, he posited, but they are also wealthy. The pitch to the Persians was that they could possess the wealth amassed by the Jews.

Haman also set up a physical destruction mechanism that was based on contemporary rituals such as the Pur—a mechanism used to determine a date on which the world would have a one-day "license to kill" the Jews and take their money.

This was the "they tried to kill us" of Purim.

Yet, Haman made one big mistake in his intelligence gathering: he was not aware that the king's wife, Esther, was Jewish—a fact she kept a secret. Thus, the "we survived" part was carried out via Esther, who used her feminine ingenuity to convince the king to put in place mechanisms to reverse Haman's plans. Indeed, the day that had been meant to be the end of Judaism has become a festive one for the Jews—Purim. To mark it, Jews eat "HamanTash"—pastries resembling the ears of Haman.

The Jews survived, rebuilt Jewish life in Judea, and indeed rebuilt the Temple. The Persians resumed their long-lasting friendship with the Jews, but they were soon to lose their global dominance.

The 3rd century BC marked a historic shift of global power from the Middle East to Europe. For centuries, global ethos was dominated by Middle Eastern empires—Egypt, Assyria, Babylonia, and Persia. Suddenly, power shifted westwards—first to the Greeks, then to the Romans. Indeed, Europe was soon to become the dominant global power for the next two thousand years, till the 20th century CE, when power shifted westward yet again, this time to the United States.

The shift began with Greece's gradual defeat of Persia's reign over its 127 provinces, including Judea. The Greek invasion of Judea ended a few centuries of renewed prosperity for Jews in Judea and marked the beginning of the 2,300-year-old European-Israeli conflict—the world's oldest conflict, which is still a driving force for much of today's geopolitics, as well as the assault on Judaism. (For more on this subject, see my analysis on: EuropeandJerusalem.com.)

GREEKS (HANUKKAH)

Unlike previous invaders of Judea, and the Biblical wars fought against Israel, the Greeks were not as interested in land, taxes, or deporting the Jews. They were interested in ending Judaism—to un-Jew the Jews by forcing "European values" on them.

While Persia's ultimate path-to-destruction was to kill Jew-by-Jew, the Greeks opted for a collective group elimination—to end the idea of Judaism. Both attempts had physical and ideological components that worked autonomously from each other. In Persia's case, the buildup of an ideological characterization of Jews as a pariah supported the destruction though physical means—killing Jew by Jew, as the Book of Esther states: "to destroy, to slay, and to cause to perish, all Jews."

With the Greeks, the dynamic was reversed: Physical murder of non-compliant Jews, at times en masse, was just the supporting act to the final goal of eradication. The destruction was committed through an ideological attack on Judaism. This assault on Judaism was carried out through the erasure of all traces of Jewish life, which to a large extent was anchored in the Temple.

The Greeks targeted the Temple by going in, desecrating it, and placing their idols in it. In addition, they prohibited Jewish rituals such as circumcision, and at the same time promoted "European values" to the Jews, including body-worshiping, promiscuity, Greek culture, and entertainment. This was done, of course, to "benefit" the Jews, or so they were told.

The Jews ungraciously rejected the European invader's generous effort to enlighten them. They refused to abandon their values, their particularity, their ideology, their pride in their national identity, and mostly their faith in God. The Greeks then upped the physical attack to enforce the ideological path-to-destruction of Judaism—this was the "they tried to kill us" component.

Just as Haman had miscalculated the power of one woman, Esther, through whom the Jews were saved, the Greeks underestimated the conviction and determination of one family, the Maccabim, who led a coup. Eventually the Maccabim defeated the Greeks, liberated the Temple, purified it, and invited the priests to once again light the Menorah with sanctified oil.

We survived, and, to mark it, Jews eat oily latkes on Hanukkah, to represent the oil that was miraculously sufficient to light the menorah.

ROMANS (TISHA B'AV)

Jews enjoyed sovereign life in their land once again, but soon came another European invader, the Romans, and like the previous European occupier and those who were to come, they attempted to negate Judaism.

The Romans eventually destroyed the Temple, deported the Jews from Jerusalem, and then from Judea. Most Jews—whether as slaves or as refugees—made their way to Europe, where for the next two thousand years, they lived under European persecution.

Indeed, it is quite amazing that Judaism was able to survive the Roman deportation. This is a unique phenomenon in history, as other nations that were deported from their homeland and lost their anchor, eventually evaporated. Judaism survived by going through a historic transformation: synagogues replaced the Temple, structured prayers replaced sacrifices, insular life in the Jewish ghetto replaced insular life in Judea, and the ritualistic yearning to return to Zion replaced the physical presence in Jerusalem. This transformation from Judaism 1.0, anchored in the physical presence in Judea and worship in the Temple, into Judaism 2.0, anchored in insular life in exile and strong religiosity, is what enabled the unlikely survival of Judaism.

But just as Judaism evolved, so did the European opposition to Judaism. This was not clear at first, since in one of history's most stunning reversals, the invader who tried to impose "European values" on the Jews, eventually succumbed and accepted "Jewish values" in Europe. Indeed, the Romans brought Jewish Monotheism into its empire in the form of Christianity—so metaphorically, instead of Europeanizing Judea, Europe was Judaized.

But European opposition to Judaism did not end, it just evolved. With this new set of circumstances, European opposition was channeled through religious Christian frameworks. During the next two thousand years, Europe would engage in multiple large-scale assaults on Judaism in an attempt to eradicate it.

Once again, those assaults included both an ideological and a physical component. Once again, the physical and ideological assaults were interdependent. Once again, Europe used destruction mechanisms that were the most effective for that period, deployed by the most powerful entity possessing such mechanisms.

One place in which Jews thrived was the Iberian Peninsula of Southern Europe—today's Spain. During what is known by historians as the "Golden Age" of Judaism, Jewish residents of Spain lived for centuries side-by-side with the Muslim residents of Spain.

SPAIN

The 15th century assault on Judaism started with an invasion, a conquest, and a war that seem to have nothing to do with the Jews—when Europeans invaded the Iberian Peninsula and ended centuries of Muslim rule. To Muslims' chagrin, this is described in Spanish textbooks and history classes today as the "Re"-conquista (or reconquest), based on a theory—that the invaders who conquered Spain, are loosely connected to those who lived there one thousand years ago.

Ferdinand and Isabella, the king and queen completing the *Reconquista*, moved on to launch an attack on the Jews. That attempt to eradicate Judaism was staged, once again, through dual tracks. One track involved deporting Jews who agreed to leave voluntarily. (They were ordered to leave Spain by Tisha B'Av—the holiday marking the destruction of the Temple and deportation of Jews from Judea.) The other track, we now know, amounted to murdering those who stayed, through a creative new technique.

One could stay, but only if one converted to Christianity. Once Christian, Jews were under the auspices of the Inquisition. The Inquisition represented the Catholic Church, and hence only had jurisdiction over Christians. It was that Inquisition that then proceeded to murder the (former) Jews.

Here too we see both an ideological and a physical component: The narrative that was instilled was that those "new Christians" continued to practice their Judaism. They took advantage of the provisions that allowed them to stay in Spain by converting to Christianity but cheated and continued to be Jewish. Jews once again were accused of being rule-breaking pariahs, opposed by the rest of the world.

The physical actions of the Inquisition likely got public support due to that narrative, in addition to the practical aspects that those Jews (a.k.a. "new Christians") were now competing with Europeans.

Judaism was not meant to survive the 15th century attempt to eradicate it—Jews would either be murdered, converted to Christianity, with the knowledge that passing any traces of Jewish identity to their descents could result in their murder, or deported and evaporate into the world's nations. But Jews survived. They came to Eastern Europe, Morocco, and even Palestine (the name given to Judea by the Romans after they deported the Jews—named for the Jew's Biblical arch-rival, the Philistines, by then long-extinct).

The deportation that was meant to eradicate Judaism led to the thriving and expansion of Judaism, exactly as the actions of Pharaoh are described in the book of Exodus: "But the more they tortured them, the more they multiplied and the more they spread."

A few centuries later, in the 20th century, it was indeed the Jews' success that led to the next attempt to eradicate Judaism.

GERMANY AND THE HOLOCAUST

Unlike the Spanish attempt in the 15th century, and the Greek attempt in the 2nd century BC, when the effort to eradicate Judaism was attempted through collective elimination, targeting the idea of Judaism, the Germans of the 20th century used the one-by-one method.

This destruction mechanism took advantage of modern-day technology, such as trains, which were not available a century before. Advancements in chemistry and other sciences enabled the Germans to centralize their eradication effort through gas chambers and extermination camps.

The destruction mechanisms chosen by the Germans were also suitable for the Jewish realities of the time. Deportations of Jews, such as those employed by Spain, France, and England, led to Jews in the 20th century living in concentrated areas. Not only were more than 80 percent of Jews in Europe, but also, about 70 percent of all European Jews lived in Eastern Europe—in Poland and the adjacent parts of the Soviet Union.

Mostly, the physical assault on Judaism was enabled by the presence of the independent ideological assault on Judaism. The relatively new antisemitism movement had been gaining popularity in Europe during the end of the 19th and early 20th century, and it served as a crucial enabler in carrying out the Nazis' goals.

The 20th Century Ideological Assault on Judaism

Throughout the Middle Ages, Europe had been a religious society. Therefore, opposition to Judaism was expressed in religious terms. As discussed, the liquidation of Spanish Jewry in the 15th century was likely sold to the Spanish public as an expression of their religious faith. After all, it was carried out by the Catholic Church, which was broadly accepted as the religious authority.

Yet, by the 19th century, much of Western Europe had turned secular. The French Revolution that shaped Europe was not only based on extreme secularism, but also antitheism. Antitheism was so zealous that the revolution even attempted to change the seven-day week to a ten-day week, merely to refute the idea that God created the world. Europe turned secular rapidly, and by the mid-19th century, many concluded that the age-old concept of European Jew-hatred was over: if European hatred was based on the religious aspect of Judaism, and Europeans no longer cared about religion, then there was no longer a reason to hate the Jews.

This view was not just theoretical, it had validation on the ground. Jews in Western Europe experienced a dramatic improvement in their fortunes as the 19th century progressed: For the first time, Jews in the West were given emancipation—they were no longer limited to the ghettoes, they were no longer prohibited from entering big cities, and no longer limited in their travel. After two thousand years, they were finally free! Moreover, Jews were no longer confined in what professions they could work in and what leisure activities they could enjoy. Jews were allowed in the cafes, restaurants, opera, and concert halls. At last, Jews were allowed to be French, to be German.

Therefore, the prevailing wisdom towards the end of the 19th century was that Jew-hatred was over and it was a new world. Jewish philosopher Moshe Hess wrote in his 1862 book, *Rome and Jerusalem*, that the declining power of the Vatican and the pope would lead to a new era for the Jews: "With the revival of Italy, will come the revival of Judea." Other Jewish writers, such as Stefan Zweig, viewed themselves as Europeans, loved their Kaiser and their empire, and could not imagine a world other than the benevolent world they lived in.

But the emancipation of the Jews also triggered a European counter-reaction. And that is understandable. Suddenly, Jews were competing with the "indigenous" Europeans for jobs. Jewish businessmen were taking market share from Europeans' businesses. Being allowed out of the ghetto was one thing, but full rights?

In addition, Europeans had been indoctrinated for centuries to believe that the Jews were the "suffering remnant," that they were poor and miserable because of their sins and would stay like that for as long as they stayed Jews. (European Christians only shifted away from that to fully embrace the Jews in the late 20th century).

Even as Europeans became secular, such a core view likely stayed somewhere in the depth of their consciousness. So how could Jews be successful, and what did it say about "us, the Europeans," the new "chosen people," if the Jews who are supposed to suffer, now thrive, and do so on our land, at our expense?

By the end of the 19th century, Jews had amassed significant wealth and power. The Rothschild family, for example, controlled a banking empire. Jews also penetrated government and were involved in massive European projects—from the Panama Canal to the building of railroads. The "Jewish occupation of Europe" led to a new form of opposition to Judaism: opposition to the emancipated Jew. Toward the end of the 19th century, this popular movement was given a new name: antisemitism.

While today we use the term antisemitism to describe Jew-hatred as a whole, at that time it was a specific genre of opposition to Judaism. (Similarly, today we use anti-Zionism and Israel-bashing to discuss a particular opposition to Judaism, but that too could soon be the new term to describe Jew-hatred as a whole.)

Indeed, at first, there had been widespread dismissal of the idea that antisemitism is a form of Jew-hatred or any form of hatred—rather, it was considered legitimate criticism of Jewish behavior. Similarly, at first, antisemitism was not viewed as an ideology that could develop into a substantial threat to Judaism or to individual Jews. Sure enough, some antisemites genuinely claimed that they were friends of Jews, and wished to reform them for their own sake. Some Jews had antisemitic acquaintances, and perhaps "agreed to disagree" when it came to politics and the "Jewish Question." One of the most popular books in France in the 19th century was Édouard Drumont's *Jewish France*. It influenced not only hard-core antisemitics, but also antisemitic-lites who merely wanted to "end the occupation"—to go back to a Europe that had less Jewish influence in government, business, culture, music, and society. Indeed, as the 20th century progressed, antisemitic ideology became deeply ingrained in mainstream European consciousness.

While the ideological assault on the Jews in Germany, France, and throughout Europe escalated through the early part of the 20th century, it did not possess destruction mechanisms.

Antisemitism was "just" an ideology, a political view, and a way to express frustrations. Moreover, Jews felt safe because they believed that governments would protect them.

After all, it is not the antisemitic masses on the fringe who control the destruction mechanisms against Judaism, it is governments, and while governments might do things that would upset the Jews, they would never allow the Jews to be targeted physically. And so the antisemitic ideology that was born in the mid-19th century in reaction to the emancipation of Jews and that got its name in the 1870s matured toward the turn of the 20th century into a populist movement—yet without a destruction mechanism.

When an actor appeared on the European stage who possessed the destruction mechanism—the German Nazi party—the ideology was already there, deeply rooted in the European consciousness, and ready to use.

The 20th Century Physical Assault on Judaism

Indeed, as the Germans were set on conquering Europe, country by country, they likely realized they might find much-needed allies in the target countries.

Germany was ready to rid the world of Jews. Antisemites throughout Europe were interested as well. As discussed, the antisemitism ideology was deeply entrenched but did not have destruction mechanisms.

So in comes an invader who does have destruction mechanisms, has activated them, and is now using them. On the one hand, the Germans were brutal invaders and occupiers, but on the other hand, the thinking went, they might ultimately improve conditions by killing Jews. Antisemites in European countries had been warning about the Judaizing of their country for years.

The day had come to finally address it. Indeed, as the Germans moved forward in their conquest of Europe, many Europeans throughout the continent chose to collaborate with the Germans by arresting Jews and delivering them to the Nazis.

And thus, a fifty-year-old ideological assault on Judaism met a physical assault by the Nazis. The two recurring themes in the assaults on Judaism—European collaboration, and interdependence between ideological assault and physical assault—were very much present. The successful instilling of the antisemitic ideology had a twofold effect. It gave rise to the Nazis who executed their mission to eradicate Judaism, and it provided flocks of collaborators for the Nazis as they conquered Europe, gaining access to more and more Jewish communities, which the Nazis in turn liquidated. In just a short four years, a third of the world's Jewish population was murdered.

The "they tried to kill us" part of Tisha B'Av includes both the Roman deportation of Jews from Judea and the Spanish deportation, which occurred on the same day, some fourteen hundred years apart. The "they tried to kill us" of Holocaust Remembrance Day is t2he German-led attempt.

In all three cases, the "we survived" part did not come right away. It only came in 1948, when the Jewish state was reestablished, ending two thousand years of exile. Zionism—the national movement of the Jewish nation-religion launched by Theodor Herzl in 1897, just fifty years earlier—proved to be the salvation of Jewish life. Zionism was the "we survived" part, and the role played by one individual, Queen Esther, during Purim and a family, the Maccabim, during Hanukkah, is now played by the entire Jewish nation.

The Jewish state was able to sustain formidable economic, security, and social challenges as it gathered Jews from the four corners of the world and eventually became a home for nearly half of the world's Jewish population. By the 21st century, the Jewish state reached new heights of success, becoming one of the world's largest economies and possessing one of the stronger and savvier militaries. There are many political differences, vocal disagreements, and passionate arguments, but Zionism remains the uniting ideology. Over 99 percent of Israel's Jews vote for Zionist parties, and no matter which side of a debate they are on, protesters march with the Zionist flag of Israel, while each side states that their fight is for the sake of Zionism.

Indeed, by the 2020s Judaism has been going through a historical transformation, with Zionism turning into its anchor. Whether it is in positive or negative contexts, Zionism and the Jewish state have become the primary touch-point with Judaism for most Jews and non-Jews alike. It is therefore only logical that the new assault on Judaism is being pursued through the prism of Zionism.

CHAPTER 2

TODAY'S ATTEMPT: ISRAEL-BASHING

Over the last few years, Judaism has once again been under an ideological assault. As in all previous attempts to eradicate Judaism, the assault is carried out through the most relevant aspect of Judaism. In our time, it is Zionism.

The establishment of the Jewish state in 1948 provided the Jew-basher with a tangible platform to attack. This was only amplified by the astonishing success of Israel in the 21st century—economically, militarily, in society, and in its contribution to humanity. Suddenly, the Jew-hater, in search of a vehicle through which to attack the Jews, was given the perfect target: A Jewish state, which is successful and houses the plurality of world Jewry. This is something the Jew-haters did not have during the prior two thousand years when they had to attack amorphous bodies such as "rich Jews," "disloyal Jews," or "Jews who said they converted to Christianity but secretly practiced Judaism."

Till now the Jew-hater had to resort to extreme creativity in his incitement against the Jews: "one of the ingredients for those Matzos they eat on Passover is the blood of Christian children," "they walk around at night and poison the wells," or "they starve European children as a way to take over Europe" and "get together for secret meetings where they plan to take over the world" (and even keep protocols of their plans). All of those were sufficient to incite the world against the Jews and were the basis for past attempts to eradicate Judaism.

Now, it is so much simpler: "The Jews kill Palestinian children as they try to take their land." That is a much more relatable accusation. After all, Europeans have been doing that since the beginning of European times. Similarly, "the Jews engage in ethnic cleansing"—that too has been a European pursuit. Indeed, a large collection of relatable and tangible accusations that are directed at the Jewish State makes it much easier in our day to incite against the Jews.

Israel-bashing is a relatable and user-friendly ideology, which now plays the leading role in the age-old opposition to Judaism. This is especially the case since the last ideology that played a leading role—antisemitism—is no longer user-friendly. Social realities and the shock of the Holocaust make it taboo to be outright antisemitic. Directing hate to Judaism through antisemitism is prohibited. Yet redirecting your hate through Zionism and the Jewish state is allowed.

To state the obvious, Zionism is not the reason for the assault on Judaism. It is just the vehicle through which the assault is being carried out, and that is because it has become the most relevant aspect of Judaism.

THE TRANSFORMATION OF JUDAISM

The story of Judaism is simple: The Jews lived in Judea (Judaism 1.0), they were forced into two thousand years of exile where they developed a different modus apparatus that allowed them to weather the years of exile (Judaism 2.0), and now the Jews are back in Israel, and Judaism has a new organizing principle—Zionism (Judaism 3.0).

Zionism has become the most relevant aspect of the Jewish nation-religion, and this is happening without any compromise to the religious aspects of Judaism. Whether positively or negatively, this is where a Jew meets his Judaism and the outside world meets the Jews. While Zionism is defined quite simply as the national expression of the Jewish nation-religion, the mere mention of the term triggers emotions both good and bad. No other aspect of Judaism evokes such a degree of passion, anger, love, fear, pride, dissent, and, indeed, engagement. This underscores that Judaism has transformed and Zionism is now its anchor.

Therefore, contemporary opposition to Judaism is expressed through anti-Zionism and Israel-bashing.

Theodor Herzl, the father of today's Zionism, predicted exactly that.

Herzl

Herzl was part and parcel of the European elite in the 1890s. He was a playwright and a journalist, holding one of the most influential positions in European media: the Paris bureau chief of the *Neue Freie Presse*, one of Europe's leading liberal newspapers—perhaps akin to today's *New York Times*.

Herzl was Jewish, but many in his social circles truly believed that this no longer mattered. The prevailing wisdom held that Jew-hatred was over. It belonged to past centuries when Europe was religious and opposed Judaism for religious reasons. But Europe was now secular, enlightened, and liberal, and the Jews had been emancipated.

So, when a new form of opposition to Judaism emerged, later dubbed antisemitism, many Europeans argued that this was not a form of Jew-hatred, but merely a "political view" about the "Jewish Question." Herzl studied the matter and reached a different conclusion. European opposition to Judaism was permanent and chronic, he posited, and it evolved to fit changing European and Jewish circumstances. Moreover, Herzl understood that there was no point in trying to persuade Jew-haters. He mocked "committees against antisemitism" that were forming at that time since one cannot convince dogmatic minds. The only way to address European Jew hatred would be through a paradigm shift, he argued, and that paradigm shift would be the establishment of a Jewish state.

A Jewish state would be the correct interface to address European opposition to Judaism. Moreover, innovations produced in the Jewish state, once Jews were free, would advance humanity to unimaginable levels. He wrote: "The Jewish state will exist because it is the necessity of the world." (Herzl championed the concept we call today "peace through strength.")

Moreover, Herzl understood that in two thousand years of exile, Judaism had come to be defined by European opposition to it. Jews were like a lion thrown into the sea. Naturally, the lion develops fins to survive and comes to be viewed as a marine animal. Indeed, who today views a sea lion as a lion? Jews, Herzl argued, are no longer "organic Jews." Their behavior and thinking, and even physical attributes (such as being timid, weak, and bent-down) are because they are in the sea of European persecution. Therefore, just as a sea lion cannot come out of the water and just reenter his former habitat, the jungle, and survive, Jews could not just move back to their ancestral homeland and expect to survive.

Just as the lion needs to go through a transformation, so did the Jews, and the vehicle for that transformation would be Zionism. Indeed, Herzl mocked ideas to "just do it," to just get on boats and head home, because once there, Jews would realize that they had lost the uniting force of European opposition.

Herzl studied Moses, who, in his interpretation had not merely led a journey from Egypt to Canaan. The journey had served as a tool to transform the nation. Herzl called it "Education through immigration," and he vowed to transform the Jewish nation through immigration once again.

In Moses's time, however, there had been Jews who did not transform. Their thinking was still filtered through the perspective of Egyptian enslavement. Similarly today, there are Jews who have remained mired in the legacy version of Judaism, and their thinking is filtered through the perspective of European enslavement. It should be no surprise that those untransformed Jews attacked Moses's Judaism back then, and that it is those untransformed Jews who attack Herzl's Zionism today.

But as a student of Moses, Herzl anticipated this opposition: "We shall have to endure hard and bitter struggles: with regretful Pharaohs, with our enemies, and above all with ourselves."

He also understood that Zionism would not only become the vehicle to emancipate Jews physically from Europe and their various diasporas and bring them home, but would be the ideological infrastructure that would transform Jews and allow them to prosper once home:

"There are those who do not understand us properly and believe that the purpose of our effort is to return to our land," Herzl said in a speech in 1899. "Our ideal goes well beyond that. Our ideal is the vision of grand eternal truth; it is an ideal that always moves forward; it is an ideal that is infinite, that forever grows, in such a way that with every step forward that we take, our horizon expands in front us, and in its perspective, we see an even greater and more noble purpose to which we strive."

Herzl launched the Zionist movement at the First Zionist Congress in 1897 in Basel, Switzerland, where he declared that "Zionism is the return to Judaism, even before it is the return to the Jewish state." In Zionism, Herzl created a new organizing principle of Judaism. "We got Judaism in our hands," he said.

Herzl understood though that the recognition of this will take time. Indeed, it is only in the 2020s that the transformation he seeded is becoming evident. There were hurdles in the way in Israel's first seventy years—Zionism's over-association with secularism, for instance, but with a shift of power and Zionist ethos from the secular minority to the religious/traditional majority and a religious rapprochement amongst Israeli seculars, that and other hurdles are now removed.

Herzl predicted that opposition to the Jews would follow them wherever they go. Now that both Jews and Judaism are back in Zion, the underlying hatred has indeed followed and is expressed as opposition to Judaism through Zionism. Like the antisemitic ideology that was developed in the 19th century in response to the Jews' emancipation and success, a new ideology, has evolved in the 21st century in response to the establishment of the state of Israel and its extraordinary success: Israel-bashing.

Just as it took a few decades for the antisemitic ideology to mature into the vehicle of attempted eradication of Judaism (from the late 19th century to the mid-20th century), so has it taken the Israel-bashing ideology a few decades to mature into the ideology under which the contemporary assault on Judaism is carried. (The more common term used today is anti-Zionism, but the more precise term is Israel-bashing, which includes even those who identify as Zionists, but still bash Israel. For practical purposes, those two terms can be used interchangeably. There were various terms in the late 19th century to describe the new form of opposition to Judaism of the time, such as Israel-eaters, until it was settled that the common term is antisemitism, even though that is not precise either).

ISRAEL-BASHING TODAY RESEMBLES ANTISEMITISM OF THE EARLY 1900S

The early stages of antisemitism bear an eerie resemblance to the early stages of Israel-bashing, though it is clear that Israel-bashing of the 2020s is far more advanced and poisonous than antisemitism was in the early 1900s. Both movements were rather amorphous at first. There was no central command or hierarchy; there was no membership card.

Just as some back then went so far as to suggest that antisemitism is not a form of Jew-hatred, but merely a vehicle to reform the Jews, the same case is made today. Many Israel-bashers explain that they are doing this for Israel ("we love Israel, but not when its military operates in Gaza"), and more extreme anti-Zionists even stretch the human mind by saying they love Jews but hate Zionists.

Similarly, there was a debate about the line between "legitimate criticism" of Jews and outright antisemitism, just as there is debate today over the line between criticism of Israel and outright Israel-bashing.

Back then, there were accusations that Jews brought it upon themselves: They amassed too much power; they speculated in the stock market; they bought coal mines and reduced safety standards, dwelled in the cafes of Europe, and were just too visible—they chose to engage in a Jewish occupation of Europe. Today, there are accusations that Jews brought it upon themselves: They violate international law, commit war crimes, build settlements, built a wall around Gaza, and once again, engage in occupation.

Back then, Herzl and cosmopolitan Jews had friends or acquaintances who were antisemitic. One of them, French author Alphonse Daudet, even brainstormed with Herzl about the best ways to advance his Zionism vision, urging Herzl to write a novel, rather than a manifesto, to reach a broader audience (Herzl ended up doing both—first a manifesto, *The Jewish State*, and then a novel, *Altneuland*.) Today as well, many of us have friends or acquaintances who are Israel-bashers. It is impossible to be a journalist, artist, professor, or actor, without having such colleagues.

Herzl said he developed a "liberal attitude" towards antisemitism back then, and many of us "look the other way" or "agree to disagree" when encountering Israel-bashing. Indeed, just like antisemitism was viewed as a legitimate political view, today Israel-bashing is considered a legitimate "political view."

Moreover, back then there was an obsessive focus on the threat of yesterday (religious-based Jew-hatred), so much so that the common view was that antisemitism was not a threat to the survival of Judaism. Today as well, there is an obsessive focus on the threat of yesterday (antisemitism), so much so that the common view until 2024 was that Israel-bashing is not a threat to the survival of Judaism.

In addition, both antisemitism in the 1900s and Israeli bashing in the 2020s are socially acceptable and even fashionable. Most dangerously, both antisemitism then, and Israel-bashing today, are promoted using both media and opinion leaders, such as the French newspaper *La Libre Parole* and German opera composer Richard Wagner back then, and mainstream media and credible international organizations today.

Israel-bashing in the 2020s is the vehicle to eradicate Judaism in decades to come, just as antisemitism of the 1900s was a vehicle to eradicate Judaism in decades to come. While we do not know where the Israel-bashing ideology will take us, we do know that antisemitic ideology matured to be the foundation for the Holocaust that killed about a third of the world's Jewish population. While today's Israel-bashing and last century's antisemitism are eerily similar, the path to destruction going forward is different. To be able to defend against the assault on Judaism, we need to have an understanding of that path, and not just assume as human nature dictates, that the path would be the same as the last attempt to eradicate Judaism.

THE PATH TO THE DESTRUCTION OF JUDAISM

As mentioned, every attempt to eradicate Judaism uses destruction mechanisms that are the most effective for that period. The 20th century's attempt to eradicate Judaism involved killing Jew-by Jew. Such a method is irrelevant today.

The marchers in Charlottesville in 2016 yelling "Jews will not replace us" could certainly lead to violence against Jews, but they have no ability to round up Jews and kill them. So-called "right-wing antisemitism" does not possess the mechanism to eradicate Judaism that it did in the 20th century. There is no ability to gather the Jews in Hollywood, New York, and all over America, take them to extermination camps, and kill them.

Similarly, there is no risk of a Western government giving Jew-haters a "license to kill" all Jews in one day, as was the case in Persia as recounted in the *Book of Esther*. While the risk of violence and murder of individual Jews certainly exists, there is no risk of that amounting to the destruction of Judaism through killing Jew-by-Jew, as was the case in Europe in the previous century.

The path-to-destruction of Judaism today is through collective elimination, as it was in the 2nd century BC when the Greeks tried to eradicate Judaism and as it was in the 15th century when the Spanish tried to eradicate Judaism. Contrary to popular perception, this was the path-of-destruction that was launched on October 7th when Hamas killed twelve hundred Jews in one day. The path set on October 7th was not of Hamas and its partners proceeding to kill the rest of the Jews. Rather, their actions were the enabler of a path set by the West for the eradication of Judaism:

Destruction Mechanisms

Jews of the 2020s *should* feel the safest they have ever felt. Not only has the world become more tolerant, safe, and, to use Stefan Zweig's words, more like "the world of security," but many of the people who tried to kill us for centuries are now our friends.

Indeed, not only is Germany a strong ally of the Jewish state and a friend of the Jewish people, but so are all European countries. England, which once slaughtered and then deported the entirety of its Jewish population is now a friend of Israel. Spain, which deported and slaughtered Jews, is now an ally of Israel, and so are other European countries, once so adamantly opposed to whatever form Judaism took. The path to the destruction of Judaism does not lie through the direct action of those governments against individual Jews. Yet at the same time, those governments have empowered multinational organizations and given them lethal mechanisms that could be deployed toward the eradication of Judaism. For example, the International Criminal Court is funded by Europe and housed there. It has the capability to deliver paralyzing blows to Israel's security, economy, and society by threatening to arrest Israeli government officials, military personnel, and settlers—in short, all Israelis.

Other multinational structures—from the UN to ad-hoc coalitions—have other capabilities such as defunding, boycotting, blacklisting, divesting, and sanctioning Israel and Israeli Jews. Such mechanisms were instrumental in eliminating other "pariah states" such as South Africa and Ba'athist Iraq, and could in theory be deployed against the Jewish state, which, after all, is deemed by credible organizations, such as Amnesty International, to be an apartheid state that commits war crimes and crimes against humanity.

Until October 7, 2023, the danger of Israel-bashing becoming the ideology for the destruction of the Jewish state seemed as absurd as the threat of antisemitism becoming the ideology for the genocide of European Jews in the early 1900s. Friendly governments would not fulfill the threat.

Even if multinational organizations attacked Judaism, those European governments would not comply. If the ICC issued arrest warrants against Israelis, friendly governments would ignore them; if others tried to sanction Israeli Jews, Israel's allies would not comply. This was the prevailing view on September 2023.

Israel-Basher-Lites

The potent part of the existential threat to Judaism does not lie with the aggressive vocal elements of the Israel-bashing movement, such as the pro-Palestinian demonstrators waving "From the river to the sea" banners, since they do not have the destruction mechanisms. The lethal threat comes from the "polite"

Israel-basher-lites—mainstream people in the UN, other multinational organizations, the media, foreign offices, treasury departments, and even world leaders.

Those are not self-described Israel-bashers or anti-Zionists, but they are influenced by popular Israel-bashing sentiments. Herzl understood that even well-intentioned world leaders would be vulnerable under such circumstances: "Even if we were as near to the hearts of princes as are their other subjects, they could not protect us. They would only feel popular hatred by showing us too much favor."

Similarly, just as previous large-scale assaults on Judaism originated from the most powerful entity that possessed such destruction mechanism—be it Persia, Greece, Rome, The Vatican, Spain, or Germany—today such an assault is launched from multinational organizations.

Multinationalism is a new concept. There were always treaties and alliances, but it is only in recent years that such entities are getting more and more power and have outgrown their "creators"—the countries that enabled their existence. As in the idea of "machines taking over," these entities are becoming autonomous, powerful, and can now act even against the countries that created them. Such is the case with the International Criminal Court, the International Court of Justice, and various human rights organizations.

While friendly governments may not attack Judaism in our day and age, those governments are no longer in control. Suddenly, the fate of Judaism is hanging by a thread controlled by a few dozen autonomous bureaucrats, who make it no secret what they wish to do to the Jews.

Some are assured by the reality that multinational organizations are not the only powerful actors in town. Arrests, sanctions, and other nightmare scenarios can only be effective with the cooperation of the United States, Israel's steadfast ally. But as will be discussed in the following chapters, that assumption too was shattered in the aftermath of October 7th.

Moreover, the threat of such a path to destruction seemed theoretical until October 7th, but as will be discussed in later chapters, it has since become real and imminent. The ICC and the International Court of Justice, have the theoretical ability to cripple the Israeli economy and paralyze its society. Not just by the actual issuing of unannounced arrest warrants for Israelis traveling around the world, but by the mere threat of it.

Would Israelis stop traveling outside of Israel? Not conduct business, not travel for life-saving medical treatments? Not visit relatives? Once there is an actual fear of arrest, who would want to take a chance? This is not just theoretical. It was not so long ago that there were arrest warrants issued against Jews en masse. While some Jews took the risk and stayed in countries that indeed complied with "the law" and acted on those warrants, most Jews who could get out of Europe did (sadly, only a few could), and Jews who were away did not travel to Europe. The Holocaust did not only lead to the murder of Jews but also to the crippling of Jewish society and economy.

Indeed, the path to the destruction of Judaism does not lie in the 2010s BDS movement—the campaign to boycott, divest and sanction Israel—but through the 2020s DAS campaign to demoralize Israeli and Jewish society, to lead to attrition (who wants to be Jewish if this means you will be scolded on campus?), and indeed to impose crippling sanctions that can serve a devastating blow to Israeli economy, Jewish self-confidence, and contemporary Jewish life.

NOT BDS, BUT DAS: DEMORALIZATION, ATTRITION, AND SANCTION

Such actions by the International Criminal Court and the countries executing its warrants can lead to demoralization, which, the Israel-bashers hope, can then be followed by attrition—people deciding it is not worth it to keep on fighting, and leave Israel, leave Judaism.

Suddenly, a new question sprung: "Is it all worth it?"

For two thousand years, we had no choice. We were not even presented with this question. A Jew had no way out. He could have not converted, he could have not left the Jewish Ghetto, nor left Judaism. Now that Jews finally have that option, why live in Israel with terrorism as well as constant attack by the world over just about anything we do in our day-to-day life, including our right to defend ourselves? Why be associated with that pariah opposed by the rest of the world, as Sen. Chuck Schumer insinuated the Jewish state has become? Why do it to your children?

And for Jews outside of Israel, why face the insult, danger, and social repudiation that is caused merely by a last name that could sound Jewish? Why do it to your children? Get out, leave Judaism—now you finally can. That is the underlying threat of the attrition part of the path to eradicate Judaism. Moreover, as Jews outside Israel are increasingly defined by their passive de facto association with Israel, the demoralization efforts might lead some of them to actively oppose the state of Israel. Their peaceful life in America is disrupted by the Jewish state that constantly pulls them back into their Judaism, and places them in danger.

This question of "is it worth it" is even more pertinent over the last few years, since European countries have been granting citizenship to Israeli descendants of Jewish citizens who were murdered or forced out in the previous century. An Israeli now can simply leave—not as a refugee, but as a legitimate citizen of France, Spain, and even Germany. The door out of Judaism is wide open—physically and ideologically—for Jews in Israel and around the world.

Frustrations of the Demoralizers

Only a very few Israelis are currently asking the question of "is it worth it." At this point in 2024, when sanctions and arrests are mostly theoretical, there is high morale and readiness to "fight until the end" across Israeli society. This was evident in the aftermath of October 7th, as it has been throughout Israel's history. This is despite the heavily funded outside forces that are trying to demoralize Israeli society from within—so far without success.

Israelis like to complain. "The country is going to hell" is a motto of the last seventy-six years. A skit on Israel's satirical show *Eretz Nehederet* (Wonderful Country), shows a man, watching the news, through the decades as he gets older and older, and utters the same line each time, in each decade: "The country is over." Indeed, the humorous motto of the 1960s was: "The last person out, turn off the lights." But one needs to separate sarcasm from reality.

External clinging to domestic Israeli disputes in an attempt to demoralize Israeli society has failed. Israelis argue loudly, but protect each other. The passionate debates are in the context of a "family feud" and the sense of mutual assurance is unshakable. This may not be obvious for those watching Israel media, but it is strongly evident inside a tank or armored vehicle. Israelis know to contain and eternally cherish both "the honey and the sting, the bitter and the sweet," as the popular Israeli prayer song goes.

In 2018, as the U.S. moved its embassy to Jerusalem, "experts" warned that the move would lead to large-scale terrorism in Jerusalem and bring back insecurity to all of Israel. "Is it worth it?" they asked. But the Israeli public, both left and right, overwhelmingly answered: "Yes! Absolutely. It is worth it!" Indeed, the embassy in Jerusalem opened, and Jerusalem remained peaceful and safe.

Similarly, in the 2023 dispute over the government's introduction of judicial reforms, outside forces latched on to fringe groups in an apparent attempt to make the feud violent. "Resist!" read signs on billboards, bus stops, buses, and posters all over Tel Aviv, with a fist and fire in the background.

This campaign, presumed to be sponsored from the outside, failed. Israelis certainly protested loudly with conviction and high emotion, but there was no large-scale violence. When I was in Paris a few years ago, the firefighters set Place de La Concorde and a surrounding area on fire over a labor dispute. The police fired tear gas and central Paris seemed like a war zone. None of those images were seen in Israel in 2023. Nor was there a deep social rift—it was only on the surface. This was evident by the extraordinary display of unity that came after October 7th in the battlefield and on the home front.

Israel-bashers have invested millions of dollars to demoralize Israelis, to weaken the country from within—so far without success. Thus, the risk of demoralization and attrition, at least for now, exists only in the fringes of Israeli society. That fringe, however, is heavily concentrated in the media, academia, and other centers of power, and is the primary touch-point with Israeli society for parts of the American political and media establishment.

As seen on October 7th, Israelis who were abroad came back to fight. Israelis that were in Israel stayed. Morale, conviction, and determination to fight on remain high in the core of Israeli society, as seen through the 150 percent response rate to the draft of civilians to military reserve. But could this change if suddenly heavy sanctions were imposed on Israel? Indeed, such sanctions were imposed on Russia in 2022 in connection with its war with Ukraine, building on other sanctions that have been in place since Russia's 2014 takeover of Crimea. If such sanctions could lead to a severe economic crisis in Russia, one can imagine what such sanctions could do in Israel, a much smaller economy. But worse, what would happen if sanctions were imposed on Israeli high-tech companies, entrepreneurs, soldiers, and settlers—on all Israelis? One cannot predict what effect that would have on demoralization and attrition.

This is especially the case since the ICC indictments and the International Court of Justice suits, seem to base their claims, in part, on social media posts and statements of Israeli civilians. When one goes to war, one needs to have high morale. If a tweet "Let's kill the enemy" needs to be thought through a few times before being posted, that curtails the battle spirit. This indeed could lead to demoralization. The mere idea that in casual conversation between friends, one needs to be careful, since the Europeans are watching is a throwback to the time the Jews lived in Europe in fear of the Europeans who were watching.

One of Herzl's earliest works, as the ideas of Zionism were percolating through his subconscious, was a short story he wrote about a young Jew planning to commit suicide. Right before doing that, he approaches a European police officer. Now that he is going to die anyway, he can walk over to the European and "tell him off." This, in Herzl's view, symbolized the restoration of Jewish pride, taken away through two thousand years of European suppression.

The 2024 assault on Judaism works in reverse of Herzl's story: Our speech is now curtailed, and our self-confidence is being challenged. If a WhatsApp message by a mother to her soldier son saying something like "stay safe and go get them" can be produced as evidence that the Jews planned a genocide, is the mother better off not sending it? Is she better off communicating less with her soldier son in order to protect him—not from Hamas terrorists but from the vicious ICC prosecutors? And what effect does such Jewish self-suppression have on the national morale? The mention of such questions is indicative that Judaism is under assault, and that assault is coming from the West.

The September 13, 2023 Judaism 3.0 symposium about the brewing assault on Judaism was just a few days before the Jewish New Year (Rosh Hashana), so we began the event with a toast, wishing one another a year of peace. That evening was part of a series of events, exploring different aspects of Judaism 3.0, held by the Begin Center, the national institution that celebrates the legacy of one of Israel's most revered prime ministers. The breathtaking views of Jerusalem's Old City's wall that are seen while walking in the center's lobby served as a reminder to participants of what is at stake.

Each event focused on a particular aspect of the thesis, such as how trends in Israel show that we are in Judaism 3.0, how developments among American Jewry underscore that Zionism is now the anchor of Judaism, how long-term global shifts impact the thesis, and on this specific evening: The rising threat to Judaism from anti-Zionism and Israel-bashing.

With the two hundred people in the auditorium and many more watching at home, I began the discussion by outlining the path to the eradication of Judaism. I sensed the stares of skepticism. Indeed, to many in the audience, that path seemed too far-fetched: arrest warrants for Israeli citizens by the ICC? Sanctions against Israeli high-tech companies? Confiscation of Israelis' assets? An economic siege of Jerusalem? I explained that it was more far-fetched in the 1920s to issue arrest warrants against Jews, sanction Jewish-owned companies, and confiscate Jewish people's assets than it is today. Yet, I agreed with critics that the path I outlined is theoretical. After all, it would require the cooperation of the United States and European countries, who are our allies. Still, I encouraged people to focus on capabilities and not only rely on intentions, which can change.

The event was also on the eve of the 50th anniversary of the Yom Kippur War, when Israel was stunned by a surprise attack from Egypt and Syria, an attack the Israeli military establishment at the time said had been unlikely because it was not in the interests of the Arab countries to attack. This was the so-called "conception" that was proven wrong. I reminded participants that one of the key lessons learned from the Yom Kippur War was exactly that: We do not just analyze intentions, we analyze capabilities. It is true that European countries do not have the intention to arrest Israeli Jews en masse—soldiers, settlers, and political leaders. They are our friends, but they do have the capabilities, and circumstances could change.

Little did we know how quickly those circumstances would change. The peaceful world we love was about to collapse and be replaced with a world characterized with death, grief, and mourning. The physical attack on Jews not seen since the Holocaust, was followed by an ideological attack, which turned our September 13th discussion from theoretical intellectual conversation over a superb glass of Israeli wine, to a road map to counter a clear and present danger to the survival of Judaism.

A DUAL ASSAULT ON THE JEWISH NATION (FALL 2023)

CHAPTER 3

PHYSICAL ASSAULT FROM HAMAS

The early morning of October 7th was certainly not a morning like every other.

It was not only Shabbat but also the holiday of Simchat Torah, which in Hebrew means the "Rejoicing of the Torah." It is a holiday when Jews celebrate the completion of the annual reading of the first five Books of the Bible (the Torah), and begin to read it again from the beginning—from Genesis. It is the one holiday whose name suggests happiness. Little did we know that this holiday too would be associated with "they tried to kill us."

That day—October 7th—also marked the last day of the holiday season that started three weeks earlier, right around the time we held that toast for the new year at the Begin Center. Similar toasts were held throughout Israel, wishing that the new year would bring new blessings.

It was the last day of the holidays that span from Rosh HaShanah, marking the new year, through Yom Kippur, when an estimated 80 percent of Israeli Jews fast for twenty-five hours, atoning for both personal and collective sins, asking God for forgiveness, and to be ascribed in the Book of Life. It was also the end of the holiday of Sukkot, when Jews in Israel spend a week in a temporary hut built for the occasion where they eat, dwell, and sometimes even sleep—in part to emulate what the Jews experienced coming out of Egypt, and in part to get away from the materialism of one's life at home and internalize the temporary nature of life.

The holiday, when there is no school or work, was also an opportunity to hold parties. Hundreds of young Israelis attended three overnight well-organized parties in southern Israel, the largest of which was the Nova festival.

To sum it up, the early morning of October 7th was a celebration of life, a celebration of our freedom, of our pride to be part of the nation that after two thousand years is back home, enjoying a sense of security and safety.

The sirens we heard at 6:30 a.m. throughout Israel broke that illusion. It caught all of us completely by surprise: joggers on the Tel Aviv beachfront, worshipers in morning prayers at the Western Wall and in synagogues throughout Israel, partygoers at Nova, and farmers working their land in the kibbutzim and villages near Gaza. A barrage of missiles and rockets was heading towards Israeli towns—near Gaza, far away from Gaza, to Tel Aviv and Jerusalem. At the time, as Israelis were rushing to shelter, most of them had no idea that something unthinkable was happening. Thousands of Hamas terrorists had broken through the border wall separating the Gaza Strip from Israel and headed toward the kibbutzim, Israeli towns, and the parties.

They then engaged in horrific actions the human mind cannot even imagine: murder, rape, beheading, burning of people alive, snatching babies from their mothers and putting them in ovens, gassing people in their own homes, dragging Holocaust survivors from their bed and taking over 250 Israelis into Gaza. The swarm of Hamas terrorists went kibbutz by kibbutz, party by party, home by home, family by family to murder, rape, and savage. We now know they intended to proceed much further towards central Israel, to Tel-Aviv, and Jerusalem, and would have done so if not for the astonishing bravery of those who stopped them along the way. Many terrorists proudly filmed their atrocities, and some even called their parents in the middle of the act to brag. They set ambushes along the roads that led north to safety and murdered those trying to escape. Hamas's savagery produced the highest number of murdered Jews in one day since the Holocaust.

Once Palestinian residents of Gaza learned of what was happening across the fence, some decided to take advantage of the opportunity. By afternoon, it was no longer Hamas terrorists invading Israel, but Gazan civilians who crossed over to participate in the rape, murder, and savagery, taking bounty back to Gaza, ranging from bulldozers to art, as well as their own hostages.

The terrorists—Hamas and Gazan civilians alike—took advantage of the relatively low state of national and military alert. Soldiers were on leave, and those staying on base were in holiday mode.

While Hamas terrorists killed so many, that day could have been much worse. They were stopped by the heroic actions of soldiers on duty, off duty soldiers, civilians with gun licenses, policemen, and unarmed civilians, armed only with a car, who decided to risk their lives and drive through the Hamas roadblocks into the zone of savagery to save as many people as possible.

Soldiers went above and beyond the call of duty. Male, female, young and old, Jews, Muslims, Christians, and Druze—fighting all day on October 7th in what quickly became apparent was a war for the survival of Israel and what overnight became the active front of the Western world's war against terrorism. Multivolume books can be written about the stories of such bravery—one individual saving dozens of lives, thousands of individuals saving all of Israel. The Jewish nation will forever be grateful to those who stepped up on October 7th, took the initiative, and prevented that day from becoming much worse. Some paid with their lives.

That Saturday morning in Jerusalem saw worshippers rushing out of synagogues, going home to switch from their festive holiday clothes to military uniforms, pack bags, and head to base. The roads of Jerusalem would normally have been quiet that day, since religious people do not drive on Shabbat and on holidays (this being both)—people, not cars, populate the roads. But that morning, the streets were filled with cars of soldiers on leave heading back to duty, reserve soldiers of all ages not waiting to be called up and driving to their units, and of civilians, volunteering as de facto taxi drivers, picking up soldiers and driving them to their bases.

During the next few days, entire cities, villages, and kibbutzim were evacuated in northern and southern Israel. Foreign tourists were leaving Israel, and so, the luxury hotels of Tel Aviv and Jerusalem turned into "refugee camps" for those displaced from the North and South.

As civilian refugees were making their way to central Israel away from danger, thousands of Israelis around the world made their way to the closest airport, towards danger, eager to join the fighting. There was no room on flights to Israel in the days following October 7th, but El Al, the Israel's national carrier, made room in galleys, aisles, and even by the cockpit. The Jewish nation was under attack and Israeli Jews were heading home to defend it.

My mother who was born in 1948, alongside the state of Israel, and embodied much of its spirit, would say that when someone dies, you mourn during the mourning period, but after that you get up and move on. The past, by definition has passed and cannot be changed. Now, you need to march forward. And this is exactly what Israeli society did in October 2023.

The heartbreak will not be healed, the loss will never be restored, but Israelis knew that we have to move forward—each in his own role: Soldiers who buried relatives and days later reported to duty, neighbors babysitting children whose parents were called to the army, volunteers farming fields of farmers whose foreign workers left Israel, Ultra-Orthodox, religious and secular Jews joining in special prayers for the success of the soldiers, for the release of the hostages, and for the well-being of the country, grandmothers cooking all night to make homemade food for soldiers and then driving it to bases, so soldiers could enjoy something better than military food. Residents of Tel- Aviv and Jerusalem made pilgrimages to the hotels where the refugees were housed, bringing them clothes, food, toys, and diapers— and mostly offering a hug, love, and support.

"The nation of Israel is alive—in the ups, in the downs, and in the toughest hours," went the lyric of a new song that captured the public sentiment. "We are all together, nobody here is alone."

Within days of October 7th, the civic organizations that led the protests against the government just a week prior went through a metamorphosis. Taking advantage of their structure and organizations, they established civil war rooms to facilitate the purchasing of equipment for military units. American Jews and non-Jews generously donated money and equipment, and the civil war rooms rapidly placed them in the military units.

Indeed, through such generous donations, it felt as if the world was participating as Israel manned the active front in the West's war against terrorism.

THE GLOBAL INTEREST

October 7th was a global game-changer along the lines of World War II and 9/11. In the days that followed, the world seemed to recognize that this was not just an attack on Israel and the Jewish nation, but also on humanity. In previous rounds of conflict, there was international pressure on Israel to limit its response—to be "measured" and "easy" on Hamas for the sake of global stability, and to end it after some time, even if Hamas is not defeated.

The world got destabilized on October 7th, and if there was international pressure it would have made sense that the world should pressure Israel to deliver a disproportionately lethal blow to Hamas. After all, would-be terrorists in Paris, London, Malmo, Madrid, Berlin, and throughout the world were watching. Not only were they analyzing the Hamas tactics, which can be so easily replicated in Europe, but they analyzed the Israeli response.

If Israel delivered a devastating blow to Hamas, would-be terrorists in the West would be deterred, making Europe and the world safer. Indeed, even critics of Israel recognized that this time, it was about them, their own safety, and the safety of their children.

While the world's interest on October 8th was for a decisive Israeli response against Hamas, there were other people around the world who had a different interest: The Hamas attack immediately raised fears of another one from the North, from Hezbollah, as well as from Iran, the Iraqi Shia militias, and Yemeni Houthis, and this on top of fears that Palestinians in the West Bank and even some Arabs in Israel might join the assault.

Indeed, Hezbollah began firing into Northern Israel, forcing Israelis in the north to evacuate entire cities, as well as villages, kibbutzim, and agricultural fields. Houthis in Yemen fired missiles and drones at Israel. And still, the massive follow-up attack on Israel on October 2023 that would put Israel's survival in great danger did not happen.

Israelis will forever be grateful for a key reason that such a massive follow-up attack did not occur: President Biden and his administration. Speaking from the White House on October 10th, alongside Vice President Kamala Harris, the president declared: "To any country, any organization, anyone thinking of taking advantage of this situation, I have one word: "Don't." "Don't" became the headline around the world, and Israelis on the left and right alike were grateful to the president and the American people for their support. The president subsequently sent U.S. military assets to the region to back up the firm warning.

In Jerusalem, Israelis placed a giant poster near the residence of the American ambassador with a photo of Joe Biden and the words "Thank You!"

President Biden's message was received, and the would-be actors decided not to attack Israel in the aftermath of the October 7th atrocities. This, experts agreed, had been a great application of American power and global leadership. Actors did not join— not quite yet.

The long journey from a message of "Don't" to the perceived message of "Do" took only six months. As will be discussed in coming chapters, by April the United States gave Hamas a boost by threatening to defund Israeli military units fighting them, by withholding weapons from the Israeli army, and by pressuring Israel not to "finish the job."

For a few days the message of "Don't" was joined by the rest of the globe in a virtual hug for the Jewish state, but soon it became clear that a bigger existential threat was on the horizon. As brutal as the physical assault on Judaism by Hamas had been, a bigger, more lethal, more organized assault was on its way—this one coming from the West.

CHAPTER 4

IDEOLOGICAL ASSAULT FROM THE WEST

In the days after October 7th, Israel was finally popular. The Eiffel Tower was illuminated in blue and white—the colors of the Israeli flag. So was the Brandenburg Gate in Berlin, and even 10 Downing Street projected a huge image of the Israeli flag on its brownstone facade.

The October 7th attack, the world acknowledged, was not about the settlements, not about claims to Jerusalem, not about the occupation. This was simply a brutal attack against the Jews—the worst attack since the Holocaust. Indeed, the Hamas assault shook the core assumptions of many of Israel's critics. The attack came from Gaza, from which Israel fully withdrew in 2005. Israel had given the "international community" everything it asked for. Israel dismantled all the settlements in Gaza, evacuated every military base, evicted all settlers, and even destroyed synagogues, Jewish schools, and playgrounds. All traces of Jewish life were eradicated by the Israeli military and police force. Even the dead had to leave, when Jewish cemeteries were uprooted.

Indeed, by September 2005, Gaza was Jew-free. Israel had fully complied with what it was told to do.

Ariel Sharon, the once right-wing prime minister, was welcomed in the UN with applause and shows of admiration. He quickly became the hero of the international community and a UN darling. From now on, the consensus was, nobody could possibly accuse Israel of occupying Gaza, placing roadblocks, conducting military operations, or doing anything in violation of international law in the Strip: Israel had ended its occupation of Gaza!

I remember conversations in 2005 with a few progressive friends who complimented Israel for finally doing the right thing, and assured me that if Israel was attacked from Gaza again it would have the moral high ground and the entire world would back Israel.

The term "moral high ground" was used frequently at that time. Israel gave peace a chance, and if that fails, it had the world's promise that it would support the Jewish state as it delivers a devastating blow to those attacking it from Gaza.… Indeed, during the first days after October 7th, we did not hear the usual "we-condemn-Hamas-but…" talking points. The condemnation around the world was unequivocal. This had been Israel's 9/11.

At last, the world acknowledged the sheer evil Israel was facing. At last, the world drew a proper distinction between good and evil, between victim and perpetrator. It lasted a few days.…

Veteran Israelis reminded each other that sooner or later the haters would find a way to assault Israel, to urge "restraint on all sides," to find a way to turn fair to foul and foul to fair.

WAR CRIMES NEED A WAR

While Israelis were licking their wounds and preparing to fight back, Israel-bashers in the West (who, to their credit, had condemned Hamas's attack) soon realized that a gift had tumbled into their laps.

As discussed in Chapter 2, Israel-bashers wish to eradicate Judaism through contemporary mechanisms that are available in the 2020s: Arrest warrants for Israeli soldiers, criminal investigations of political leaders, demoralization of Israeli society, attrition, and sanctions. As of 2023, these were merely on a wish list.

Indeed, Israel-bashers in September 2023, were akin to antisemites of the early 20th century. In both cases, the ideology was well-developed and included a cohesive narrative, talking points, slogans, merchandise, symbols, and culture. In both cases, the anti-Jewish poison they spread deeply penetrated Western society. Indeed, Israel-bashing today is even more deeply rooted in Western society, than antisemitism was in the 1930s.

Yet, both the antisemitism ideology of the 1930s and the Israel-bashing ideology of the 2020s needed a trigger. After all, there can be no arrests of Jews for war crimes, if there is no war. On October 7th, Hamas provided exactly that. Hamas gifted the Israel-bashers a war, and the Israel-bashers could now proceed down the path to the destruction of Judaism.

But how can one retrofit October 7th into such accusations? Some at first tried to describe the kibbutzim and villages attacked by Hamas on October 7th as "settlements."

This was rejected even by critics of Israel. Nice try, but those were within 1967 lines—not to mention that many residents of those villages and kibbutzim, including some who were murdered, were at the forefront of advocating for the people of Gaza.

Those kibbutzim and villages employed Gazan civilians (some of those employees we now know were spies who gathered intelligence for Hamas), and provided a range of help. One of the Israeli victims had volunteered for years to drive Gazans who needed medical treatment to hospitals in Israel. The "attack against settlers" narrative did not work and was discarded.

Indeed, in the days after October 7th, the world remained with Israel. But then…

UN: OCTOBER 7TH DID NOT HAPPEN IN A VACUUM

The first global leader to break ranks with the truth and resort to the good old European narrative that if something is wrong, it must be the fault of the Jews, was none other than UN Secretary-General António Guterres, who proclaimed on October 24th that "October 7th did not happen in a vacuum," thus providing the first shot in what would soon become an onslaught.

How was Secretary-General Guterres able to concoct an argument that would blame Israel for October 7th?

It went something like this: Correct, Gaza was not under occupation. The UN had acknowledged that Israel fully withdrew from Gaza in 2005. But actually, it sort of was under occupation, he rationalized, because Israel and Egypt control their borders with Gaza and refuse to let certain types of supply and ammunition in. There are no open borders or free movement in and out of Gaza, as there are between European countries, so *voila*, an occupation led to October 7th.

Secretary-General Guterres echoed a flaw that Herzl identified as existing with career politicians: consistency. Herzl understood that in a democratic system, politicians feel they must be consistent. Changing their views is not received favorably by the public and might lead to them losing their next election or being mocked by the media for "inconsistency." Therefore, per Herzl, even if circumstances change, the politician is forced to use old frameworks, since he is not actually trying to do the "right thing," but is trying to please his constituencies or get elected. After a while, the behavior becomes engrained regardless of election or media coverage considerations—consistency becomes a modus operandi.

October 7th was a dramatic change of circumstances but why should Secretary-General Guterres, engage in a "mea culpa" and retract previous anti-Israel statements by admitting the Hamas massacre was unequivocally horrific and unprovoked without any ifs, ands, or buts, when he had an alternative?

With this creative spin, the UN Secretary-General opened Pandora's Box, and allowed us to understand how nothing "happens in a vacuum." Did the Secretary-General imply that the Holocaust did not happen in a vacuum? As discussed, for years Jews were accused of dehumanizing Europeans, taking business away from them, and competing for jobs and public service positions once denied to them. For years, Jews were accused of "Judaizing Europe."

So, to use Secretary-General Guterres's words, the Holocaust did not happen in a vacuum. Does that detract from its horrors, create a justification for the Nazis' actions, or place blame on the Jews? And if actions do not happen in a vacuum, what about Spain's occupation of Catalonia and the Basque Country? And more broadly, what about Spain's occupation of Spain? (Some view Spain as occupied Muslim territory.)

Shortly after the opening shot by Secretary-General Guterres, who is from Portugal, his Iberian Peninsula compatriot, Spanish Prime Minister Felipe Gonzalez joined the attack: The response to the October 7th Hamas attack must be…a unilateral declaration of a Palestinian state, the Spanish prime minister proclaimed. Since the EU was not ready to take that stance, Spain would announce it unilaterally, he stated in November 2023.

Islamic terrorism in the Iberian Peninsula did not happen in a vacuum either. Some progressive voices in Spain are unhappy that, per their narrative, Spanish children are indoctrinated with the fable of a "Reconquista." Ferdinand and Isabella completed the conquest of Spain in the 15th century, ending one thousand years of thriving Muslim and Jewish civilization, ethnically cleansing Muslims and Jews alike, and bringing in new white settlers. Indeed, in this Woke and DEI narrative, Spain is viewed as a colony.

So does this mean that terrorist attacks carried out in the last decades by Muslim terrorists in Spain did not happen in a vacuum? It has already been four hundred years that Spain occupied the land, per the Woke narrative—during which it has not only suppressed Muslim life, but also made no attempts to reach a compromise, such as the idea of a two-state solution. Moreover, Spain has never even admitted that they took the land away. They are still referring to a Reconquista.

Indeed, it is understandable that pro-Palestinian forces want to remove the word Reconquista from textbooks and designate it as "hate speech." The idea that Spain engaged in a "Re"-conquista based on a theory that the people completing the conquest of Spain are loosely related to the people who were there over one thousand years ago, primarily through similar skin color, gives legitimacy to the more historically sound argument that Jews are returning to their ancestral homeland.

An Attack on Judaism from Spain, Again

The EU's Josep Borrell, a Spaniard, who is the "High Representative of the Union for Foreign Affairs and Security Policy," is the third member of the Iberian Peninsula "Three Musketeers." He joined the apparent scheme of "Spanish insecurity deflection" just three days after October 7th.

With terrorists still at large in Southern Israel and bodies of Israelis still on the side of the roads, Borrell apparently felt the need to state that in his opinion Israel was already in violation of international law. This was before Israeli forces even entered Gaza! Apparently, the "right" to self-defense (a right recognized by the EU) if exercised by a Jew is assumed to be a violation of international law. A few days later, on October 18th, Borrell addressed the European Parliament, stating that "the right to self-defense, like any other right, has limits."

So let's get the position of those three Iberian leaders clear: If God forbid there is another terrorist attack in Spain as there was in the last few decades, such an attack, as UN Secretary-General Guterres suggests, would not have happened in a vacuum.

The focus should therefore be on Spain's oppression of Muslims and its occupation of the Iberian Peninsula. The proper response to that attack, per Prime Minister Gonzalez, should be a unilateral recognition of a Muslim Caliphate in Spain. We did not take that action before, he could say, but now that there has been a terrorist attack, we are reminded to do the right thing: Declare a unilateral recognition of a Muslim state in Spain. And then finally, if Spanish security forces do wish to act against the terrorists who perpetrated the attack and stop them before they commit more attacks, the Spanish security forces should go easy on the terrorists since, as EU Commissioner Borrell stated, "the right to self-defense has limits." Perhaps we should issue them a fine, he could say, and even compose a letter warning them not to do it again.

Is that the message these three Spanish/Portuguese leaders want to send to the people of the Iberian Peninsula and, by extension, to all of Europe?

No worries—it is not. This is because their stance is not taken in the context of fighting terrorism or keeping the world safe. It is done in the context of the assault on Judaism.

And so the ideological assault on Judaism of 2023 began on the Iberian Peninsula, the same place the assault on Judaism was carried out five hundred years ago.

The first "bullet" fired in the 2023 assault—that Gaza is indeed under occupation—began to resonate within the next few days. Other political leaders repeated it and the media jumped on it and began pushing stories of misery in Gaza that has been going on for decades. Conversations in the West began to shift: occupation can naturally lead people to do frustrating things, and while the October 7th attack is condemnable, it could have been avoided had there not been an Israeli occupation of Gaza.

Soon the second "bullet" in the ideological assault was fired.

ETHNIC CLEANSING

Ethnic cleansing was the Western justification for Hamas's action in 2021 when Hamas fired thousands of rockets and missiles at Israel. This was done, according to the Israel-basher narrative, since seven Palestinian families were evicted from their Jerusalem apartments in a judicial dispute. The families, who had been living in Jewish-owned homes without paying rent for decades, lost their court case and were ordered to leave.

This was immediately marketed by Israel-bashers as ethnic cleansing and echoed through the gamut of "distribution channels"—from the UN to media, through social media. Ethnic cleansing is a slogan that worked well in leveraging the Hamas missile attack on Israel in the last go-round. So why not use it again?

As Israel was about to enter Gaza and fight Hamas, the Israeli army called on the Palestinian population in northern Gaza to evacuate. The Israeli Defense Forces ("IDF") created safe passageways and dropped leaflets with evacuation directions. Hamas was not happy. It needed the people to stay as human shields. After all, Hamas fires its rockets and launches its terrorist attacks from the midst of civilian populations. It operates in tunnels built below neighborhoods with tunnel entry points in mosques, apartment buildings, and hospitals. Hamas needs civilians to stay where they are.

Fighting Hamas is certainly not conventional warfare, and Israel was faced with a set of unattractive options. One, which was certainly not an option, was not to do anything and let Hamas continue to fire rockets, hold its hostages, and launch another October 7th from Gaza.

The second option was to go in, leave the civilians there, and fight Hamas on its terms. This would no doubt result in an enormous amount of civilian casualties and would make the fighting significantly less effective since Israeli forces would be constrained.

The third option was the obvious one, which was to comply with the laws of war, logic, and Israel's values and ask the civilians to leave the war zone for their own safety. This option no doubt, had a significant operational price, since Hamas terrorists were among those civilians as well as hostages, but it was an obvious choice since it allowed for the safety of the uninvolved. Indeed, Hamas tried to stop civilians from leaving, including by firing at them. Hamas once again found a de facto ally in the West: The Israel-bashing community who enthusiastically jumped on this opportunity.

Within weeks, the talking point of "Gaza was under occupation" was joined by "Israel is committing ethnic cleansing."

And so the ideological assault on Judaism was escalating. The global mindset, indoctrinated for centuries with stories of Jews' horrific doings, was now indoctrinated with new material about the Jewish state's horrific doings. Those days in late October 2023 proved that the ideological assault on Judaism cannot be defeated with logic.

It was as if the Jewish state was given an option: Choose the war crime charges you want to face. Is it the extrajudicial killing of innocent civilians or ethnic cleansing? The war crimes arraignment had been prepared long before October 7th. All that was needed was to check the box "Ethnic Cleansing" or "Extrajudicial Killing"? No worries, the "Crimes Against Humanity" box had already been checked automatically. As instilled by opera composer Richard Wagner, Jews commit a crime against humanity merely by their existence.

Either way, by the end of October, it was clear that the Jewish state was under a dual assault. The physical attack by Hamas from Gaza and the ideological assault coming from the West were independent and uncoordinated, yet interdependent.

HUMANITARIAN CRISIS

The displaced people who left the battlefield as Israel was ready to fight Hamas gave the Israel-bashers their third "bullet" in their assault on Judaism: humanitarian crisis. Indeed, the combination of displaced people, Hamas shooting at them, and Hamas stealing the aid that was intended for them *did* create a humanitarian crisis—a crisis that could be duly leveraged in the ideological assault on Judaism.

It is fair to say that neither the Israel-bashers in the West nor Hamas cares much about the people of Gaza. Still, let us not forget that nearly two decades of Hamas rule in Gaza, with full control of the school system, media, mosques, and messaging, has naturally created a population that supports Hamas and its ideology. One can debate to what degree the interests of Hamas are correlated with the interests of the people of Gaza, but experts, as well as surveys, show that support for Hamas is widespread.

Still, Israel made it clear that its fight was not with the people of Gaza, but with Hamas. Western pro-Israel advocates even tried to paint the people of Gaza as being under occupation by Hamas and should welcome Israel liberating them. The United States government echoed similar messages. (Though even if one accepts this argument, one must take into consideration the effects of "Stockholm Syndrome.")

While it is debatable how much Hamas, which launched the physical assault on Judaism, cares about the people of Gaza, there is no debate about how much Israel-bashers in the West, who launched the ideological assault on Judaism, feel about the people of Gaza. Indeed, for them, the people of Gaza are merely tools in the ideological attack on Judaism.

One need not go far, just ask the simple question: What do the people of Gaza want? Many of them want to get out.

When there is war, people flee war zones. It is human nature. This is what happened in the Syrian war, which led to an estimated five million Syrians leaving Syria. This is also what happened in the Iraq war, the war in Afghanistan, the war in Libya, the war in Ukraine, and indeed, the war in northern and southern Israel; refugees from southern Israel have fled, and refugees from northern Israel have fled too. Hamas and Hezbollah pride themselves on having already won the war. They achieved the ethnic cleansing of the Jews from northern and southern Israel. Those areas became de facto conquests of the Muslim organizations, since they are now, just like Gaza was after the 2005 disengagement, without Jewish residents.

When civilians are at war they want to flee, and luckily there are places to go. Europe welcomed over twenty million refugees from wars in recent years, according to some estimates. It remains a heavily debated issue in European politics: How many refugees can a continent of seven hundred and fifty million people and a declining birth rate take?

Refugees' labor is reportedly sought in Middle Eastern countries, from Dubai to Saudi Arabia. A severe labor shortage can deliver a devastating blow to otherwise successful economies, and in some cases taking in refugees as well as other immigrants is a win-win situation.

Israeli refugees found a warm welcome in central Israel. While displacement for all refugees is tragic, the Israeli society's ability to welcome them, house them in luxury hotels, and integrate them into local communities, schools, and social structure, made the trauma a bit easier.

Refugees wishing to flee is a human reality and a basic human right. Making the process as easy as possible for them is a basic expression of humanity. Unless, apparently, those refugees are from Gaza.

Who Is Creating the Humanitarian Crisis?

All refugees around the world are allowed to escape a war zone, except one group—the Gazans. Why is that? Why are Gazans denied the choice to stay or go? What is it about the Gazan refugees that singles them out from all other refugees?

Israel-bashers can provide the answer with a smug smile. They are needed in Gaza for the ideological assault on Judaism!

After all, how can Israel be accused of a humanitarian crisis, when the humans who wish to flee are no longer there? How can there be stories of starvation and famine in the refugee camps near the Egyptian border, if the refugee camps are no longer there and those refugees have long since crossed the border to Egypt?

Who is stopping the Gazans from leaving? The answer provided by the West, from U.S. government officials to journalists covering the war: Egypt. The Western narrative is that yes, the Gazans who wish to leave should be allowed to do so. Yes, it is a basic human right to have the choice to flee. But it is not the fault of Western governments, western organizations, the UN, and certainly not the United States—it is Egypt's fault. It is Egypt who shuts the only way Gazans can get out, and therefore it is Egypt who denies the Gazans the right to choose whether to flee a war zone or stay. This is a childish argument.

Indeed, Egypt does not want to be flooded by hundreds of thousands of Gazan refugees—that is understandable. Beyond the obvious economic and social considerations of a mass inflow of refugees, Egypt should indeed be concerned that amongst the refugees there may be Hamas terrorists. Let us not forget that for nearly twenty years, the people of Gaza have been indoctrinated with Hamas and Muslim Brotherhood ideology—in schools, media, and youth movements. The current Egyptian regime is the archrival of the Muslim Brotherhood. The regime came about via a 2013 coup against the Muslim Brotherhood government, which was then in power in Egypt. Why should Egypt agree to let in forces that would destabilize the county, promote its nemesis, and potentially commit terrorist attacks in Egypt? They should not.

But Gazan refugees are not planning to flee to Egypt, just like Syrian refugees were not planning to flee to Turkey. Turkey was the only available border. Syrian refugees fled through Turkey, not to Turkey. This is the case with Gaza's refugees: they wish to flee through Egypt, not to Egypt. The United States could have worked with Egypt to craft safe passage routes for Gazan refugees who wish to flee, as has been done in other wars.

There is a demand for those refugees in other countries; there is a border and a safe pathway; there is a good relationship between the United States and Egypt, and there is a basket of incentives that could be provided to Egypt, not to mention pressure. After all, the Egyptian economy is in bad shape, especially after the Houthis began attacking ships in the Red Sea, leading to a dramatic decline in Egyptian revenues from the Suez Canal.

Indeed, Egypt's refusal is not the ultimate reason that those Gazan refugees are denied. One needs to look to the United States and the West: Rather than work on safe passage routes, the U.S. spent its energy in the early days of the war, asking for assurances from the Israeli government that they would not encourage Gazans to leave. Secretary Blinken reportedly even came to Israel to secure such assurances. Needless to say, Israel should certainly not encourage Gazans to leave Gaza and should provide for those displaced by war, following the laws of war and of its own moral code.

But whether one likes it or not, many Gazans naturally want to flee. Secretary Blinken underscores that the people of Gaza are just like everybody else, stating in a February 8, 2024 press conference that the families in Gaza "are just like our families" who want to have a normal life. Does this normal life entail living under a Hamas regime? Does this normal life mean living in a war zone? In refugee camps? Very few families would want this. Moreover, they are the ones, like all refugees around the world, who should decide if they want to stay or go.

In robbing them of a choice, the U.S.-led West is seemingly robbing Gazans of their most basic human rights. Indeed, when the dust settles, it is possible that the Biden administration could be accused of partaking in one of the most flagrant human rights violations of our time—failing to craft a safe passageway out for those Gazans wishing to flee, leading to what the U.S. itself describes as a humanitarian crisis at the Egyptian-Gaza border. It is a crisis that could have been averted if the United States had worked with Egypt to let them out, instead of opting to do the opposite, pressuring Israel to force them to stay in.

The Arab world has noticed this. Demonstrations erupted in various Muslim countries to protest that Western countries and Egypt denied Gazans the right to leave. This is natural. If Jews in the north had been denied the choice to leave, Israeli Jews would have been up in arms. No doubt, one can make the argument that it is in Israel's strategic interest for residents of the north to stay at home, and deny Hezbollah the narrative of "Israel surrendered and its citizens fled." But Israelis care about their people. Similarly, many Muslims around the world care about the Gazans. Europe already took over twenty million refugees in recent years. There are only two million people in Gaza, the thinking goes, and not all of them want to leave—why are they being held to a different standard than other refugees escaping war? Indeed, Arabs around the world understood what Westerns who get their information from Western media do not: The humanitarian crisis in Gaza is caused not by Israel, but by the West.

Senator Bernie Sanders called Gaza "the world's largest prison camp." In fact, he and his colleagues in the Biden administration hold the keys to that prison. To apply his own words: "Fleeing a war zone is not a privilege, it is a basic human right." And it is a right denied by the West.

Just as Israel-bashers drafted Hamas, they also drafted the people of Gaza to their cause. Gazans staying in Gaza provide fuel for the ideological assault on Judaism—a humanitarian crisis, food shortage for refugees, and inevitably, more death and more suffering. While nobody should encourage Gazans to leave Gaza, nobody should deny Gazans their right to make that choice either.

Western experts believe that if given the choice, many, perhaps the majority of Gazans would flee. This is in part because, for the last seventy-six years, the West has invested an astonishing amount of money in educating the people of Gaza with a core principle: "You do not belong in Gaza!"

Over half of the residents of Gaza are reminded day in and out, that they are not from Gaza, that they are foreigners in Gaza. They are told that they are from Tel Aviv, from Haifa, from Jerusalem, and from various other places "from the river to the sea"—and that one day they will go back. Indeed most Gazans, per the Western narrative imposed on them, are refugees not because of the 2023 war, but because of the 1948 war. To instill this narrative, the west created an entity, which arguably is one of the most profound expressions of white colonialism—UNRWA.

UNRWA

The United Nations Relief and Works Agency for Palestine Refugees in the Near East (UNRWA) is a vital component in the ideological assault on Judaism. It is funded with billions of dollars from Western countries, including the United States. (Trump stopped the funding, but Biden renewed it.)

In the 1940s there were nearly one hundred million refugees around the world. There were refugees in Europe displaced from World War II, Muslims displaced from India, Hindus from today's Pakistan, refugees in Asia, in Africa. and throughout the world. There were also about seven hundred thousand Palestinian refugees and eight hundred thousand Jewish refugees displaced by the 1948 war; Israel's War of Independence.

The UN created an agency to address the misery of nearly one hundred million refugees around the world, and through the good work of the UN and the international community over the years, nearly all of those refugees found a new home and built a new life. Indeed, their grandchildren today have all but forgotten about the 1940s. But the UN decided to carve out the Palestinian issue and created a separate entity for Palestinian refugees: UNRWA. Unlike the efforts made for other refugees to alleviate and end their suffering, UNRWA's de facto objective was to perpetuate and extenuate the Palestinian's status as refugees.

To the tune of over $1.5 billion per year, UNRWA has made sure that the Palestinians remain in 1948, that they never forget 1948, and that regardless of where they live now, they should fight for their right to return to 1948.

Jewish refugees of the 1948 war were brutally ethnically cleansed from Syria, Iraq, and other countries in the Middle East where they lived for centuries, developed good relationships with the local Arabs, built businesses, and contributed to society. Within days, the property of those Jewish families was vandalized, assets were robbed, many of them murdered, and nearly all of them were forced to leave their homes. The story of the ethnic cleansing of the Jews of the Middle East in 1948 is one of great tragedy and human suffering. And yet, the descendants of those refugees are today among the world's top scientists, high-tech entrepreneurs, doctors, professors, and thinkers.

Sadly, this is not the case for the seven hundred thousand Palestinian refugees. Back then, forces opposing Judaism identified a golden opportunity to use them as a mechanism to bash Israel, and later, for the Western effort to eradicate Judaism. And so a monstrous organization was created that is financially incentivized to count more and more people as Palestinian refugees. Today it counts under its auspices millions of refugees, including the majority of Gaza's population of two million people.

While some UNRWA employees participated in the October 7th massacre, and Hamas launched missiles from UNRWA schools and facilities, it is important to note that most Westerners working in UNRWA are well-meaning. Some of them explain to me that their working in UNRWA as teachers or as relief workers is not an endorsement of the creation of UNRWA, or even of its mandate, but an opportunity to improve a given situation. This might be true, but it also allows the organization to prosper and to be used by Israel-bashers in their effort to assault Judaism.

For seventy-six years Gazans were told that they do not belong in Gaza. Now, that they want to leave Gaza, they are told that they do belong in Gaza. What exactly is the West telling its Gazan "subjects"? Go back to northern Gaza and forget what we told you for seventy-six years—that you do not belong there? Go back to Tel Aviv? That is certainly not an option. If the people flee Gaza, UNRWA will lose its clients, revenues, power, and its thirty thousand patronage job corps.

And so, the people of Gaza are blocked by the West from leaving. The Biden administration fortified this in early 2024, when it proclaimed that the proper response to October 7th was the call for the establishment of the State of Palestine. For the State of Palestine to exist, it needs Palestinians. It needs those refugees to stay right there in Gaza.

The pro-Palestinian movement in the West needs Gazans to stay, and moreover, to stay miserable. How can you blame Israel for a humanitarian crisis in Gaza if the humans left? Mostly, the Israel-bashers wishing to eradicate Judaism need the Gazans in Gaza. Therefore, unlike any other humans around the world, the choice of whether to stay or go is denied to them. They are drafted for the noble cause—the Assault on Judaism!

THE ROAD IS PAVED

And so in the days and weeks following October 7th, an ideological assault on the Jewish state was forming around three main talking points: The attack did not happen in vacuum—Israeli has been abusing the people of Gaza for years; Israel engages in ethnic cleansing; and Israel has caused a humanitarian crisis in Gaza. By instilling these fables, the road was paved for charging the Jewish nation once again with committing crimes against humanity, and via this road forging the contemporary path to eradicate Judaism.

As stated, war crimes need a war. Hamas provided the war; the rest can be left to the imaginative human mind and the propaganda machines. Nowhere was that more visible than in the Western media.

CHAPTER 5

HAMAS'S WAR DOCTRINE: DRAFT THE MEDIA TO GENERATE PUBLIC PRESSURE

Before a country or a terrorist organization launches an attack, it calculates the reaction it expects from the other side. The concept of deterrence is based on the notion that an aggressor will not attack if it knows it will suffer a devastating blow in return. In nature, a cat shows its teeth to deter a would-be attacker. In the Cold War, the theory of MAD, Mutual Assured Destruction, was based on deterrence: the Soviet Union would not launch nuclear weapons against the United States because it knew the U.S. would have enough time to do the same in response.

Europe enjoyed fifty years of relative peace in the late 19th to early 20th century. Not because France did not want to attack Germany. In fact, French society at the time was obsessed with the concept of revanchism. Social circles, the media, and political discussions all revolved around the idea that France must avenge Germany for its humiliating defeat in the 1871 war and the loss of the French territories of Alsace and Lorraine to Germany. France did not attack Germany, not because it did not want to, but because it was deterred.

France calculated that any attempt to reclaim those territories would be met by a strong German response, and France would not only be defeated but risk losing its country. Indeed, the father of the German Empire and its first chancellor, Otto von Bismarck, predicted that as soon as France felt it was strong enough militarily, it would attack Germany. Indeed, deterrence keeps the peace and prevents the enemy from attacking.

This was exactly the so-called "conception" that the Israeli national security establishment held before October 7th. "Hamas is deterred," the argument went. This view was voiced not only in security briefings, but also by experts speaking in the Israeli media, in conferences, and in meetings Israeli officials had with their American national security counterparts.

THE "CONCEPTION"—HAMAS IS DETERRED

This deterrence, the logic went, was in place because of the price Israel extracted from Hamas after its previous offensives, like the 2021 Hamas missile attacks (the one that Israel-bashers rationalized as being in-part a response to the "ethnic cleansing" of seven families after they lost a legal dispute over housing).

In that May 2021 conflict, Hamas launched over 4,300 missiles and rockets at Israeli towns and villages. In response, Israel attacked hundreds of Hamas targets from the air, killing a large number of Hamas commanders and destroying Hamas headquarters, tunnels, weapon factories, and other assets. When Israel stopped its air raids eleven days later, due to international pressure, Hamas realized that it had sustained significant damage to its infrastructure and personnel, with over two hundred Hamas terrorists estimated to have been killed.

Therefore, the argument went, Hamas was deterred from doing something like that again. This philosophy, in one form or another, governed the seventeen years of Hamas versus Israel fighting that followed Israel's unilateral withdrawal from Gaza in 2005, and Hamas's takeover of Gaza in 2007. "Mowing the grass," as it became known, was sufficient deterrence.

In short, as of October 6, 2023, the assumption was that Hamas understood that it was not in its interest to launch another round of terrorism or fire rockets at Israel since it knew that it would pay a heavy price. So if Hamas was deterred, how could it launch on October 7th, an attack of such enormous proportions? It must have predicted the Israeli response. After all, Hamas is a relatively small terrorist organization with limited military assets, while the IDF is one of the most powerful armies in the world.

HAMAS COUNTER-DETERRENCE

The answer probably lies with three key assets Hamas believed it possessed: the hostages it planned to kidnap, the Gazan civilians it planned to use as human shields, and the Western media that would generate public pressure on Israel to eventually stop its counterattack.

Absent those three assets Hamas might have felt deterred. But with three assets, Hamas developed a "cure" for deterrence.

Hostages

This is hard to comprehend, but Hamas was able to kidnap over 250 hostages and bring them to Gaza—some alive and some dead. The hostage-taking was Hamas's biggest "insurance policy."

Beyond the "usual" terrorist objective to terrorize, it provided Hamas with three strategic advantages:

-It significantly limited Israel's operational maneuvering room. Bombing targets and attacking Hamas strongholds now needed to be done with the constraint that there might be Israeli hostages there. A softer finger on the trigger in face-to-face combat inevitably leads to more Hamas victories and Israeli losses.

-It provided Hamas with a tool to attempt to force Israel to stop its counter-operation. When Hamas felt its back against the wall, it could offer to release hostages in exchange for a ceasefire, which in turn would allow Hamas to kidnap more hostages down the line. This was applied in part early in November 2023. In exchange for the release of some of the hostages, Israel agreed to a temporary ceasefire which in turn allowed Hamas to reorganize and prepare for the next rounds of war.

-It allowed Hamas to leverage domestic Israeli political rifts to its advantage. While it would take Israel years to investigate, analyze, and internalize what led to the surprise October 7th attack, one reason mentioned by experts across the board is Israel's domestic rift.

Hamas miscalculated if it thought that the vocal and often polarizing disagreements about domestic politics would tear Israeli society apart and that Israel would be too weak to face Hamas. Immediately after the October 7th attack, Israelis united, put their political differences aside, and joined forces to fight Hamas.

Yet, the hostage situation triggered a new political dispute around the question of whether the government should accept a deal to release Hamas terrorists and halt the counterattack in exchange for the return of hostages.

To understand this, we must go back to 1977, when Israel's right-wing Likud party stunned the Israeli establishment by winning the national election, ending forty years of Labor Party rule. Since the 1930s, through the 1948 independence, and until 1977, the Labor Party and affiliates held full control of the Israeli political system, government, and economy, ruling the country in a *L'État c'est nous* way.

Since 1977, with a few short interruptions, Likud has held power. This is primarily because Israel has a permanent right-wing majority. About 60 percent of its population describe themselves as either ultra-Orthodox (Haredi), religious (including the majority of the settlement population), or Traditional (somewhat akin to the American religious right). With such a religious right-wing composition, chances of defeating Likud are slim.

In addition, the secular minority is also composed mostly of "part-time religious" ("Datlaf" in Hebrew) and many of them also vote for the right. Therefore, in recent years, the attempt to win elections shifted from a traditional right versus left debate to a de facto referendum on Prime Minister Benjamin Netanyahu, of the Likud party.

The attempt to draft "soft-right" voters away from Netanyahu has been based on different reasons over the years:

- In 2011, it was the high cost of living.
- In 2019, it was Netanyahu's indictments on corruption charges.
- In 2020, it was his Covid policies.
- In 2023, it was his government's plans to institute judicial reforms.

In all those instances, an organized public relations campaign was put in place that included frequent demonstrations and other tactics to recruit such "soft right" voters and defeat Netanyahu in the subsequent election.

The 2023 demonstrations were arguably more vocal and sustained—presumably because they were heavily sponsored by U.S.-based funding and through expensive public relations firms that dictated the messages, timed the billboards, and provided the talking points.

October 7th ended this, and an emergency national unity government was formed that put non-war issues, including the proposed judicial reforms, aside. The protests naturally subsided, but by 2024, they were redirected toward the issue of the hostage deal. The same public relations firms, same leaders, and same journalists that led the previous campaign against the government's proposed judicial reforms have led the campaign for a hostage deal.

While it was not clear if a hostage deal was even on the table, accusations began to flare early in 2024 that Netanyahu was delaying such a deal, acting from self-preservation to prolong the war and keep our men, women, children, and babies in the Hamas tunnels instead of bringing them home through a deal with Hamas.

The hostages provided Hamas with a war-ending survival mechanism. Naturally, it wants a deal that would end the war, allow it to survive, reclaim Gaza, and position itself to launch more October 7ths. Did it calculate from the start that internal Israeli politics could help it achieve such a deal? We don't know, but many experts believe that the perceived domestic Israeli rift was part of Hamas's assumptions in launching the October 7th attack and kidnapping hostages.

Those hostages kidnapped by Hamas, along with the international pressure that was generated by the media, provided

Hamas an enormous amount of leverage in its quest to end the war and persevere.

Civilians as Shields

As discussed, Gazan civilians are another key asset for Hamas—they provide human shields that significantly curtail the ability of the Israeli military to act. Therefore, the call by Israel for those civilians to evacuate the urban battlefield was met with a strong Hamas reaction, including shooting Gazan civilians on their way to safety.

The civilian aspect of the Israeli-Hamas war is unprecedented and is establishing new realities in the history of urban warfare. International law, the laws of war, and international frameworks are not set up for this kind of war, where one side not only hides behind its own civilians, but whose vested interest is for its own civilians to be killed by the other side.

Nobody could have anticipated such circumstances when the laws of war were codified. Similarly, nobody could have anticipated a bizarre reality where you have two parties, in this case Hamas and the Western Israel-bashers, who not only draw an enormous benefit from the other side mistakenly killing civilians but also rely on this happening to achieve their objectives.

Hamas's objective is for Israel to mistakenly kill Gaza civilians in its fight against Hamas. This would turn up the pressure of the international community on Israel, forcing Israel to stop and deliver Hamas the victory. This was a repeated theme during the seven rounds of Hamas versus Israel fighting over the last seventeen years, and it is the case in this war. For example, in May 2024, Hamas was entrenched in Rafah, its last stronghold. For months, Israel was under international pressure not to go into Rafah—not to "finish the job" and obliterate Hamas. This was due primarily to the presence of over a million Gazan refugees in Rafah who had escaped northern Gaza and other areas.

Pressure on Israel has come from the other side as well—why not finish the job, go into Rafah, and obliterate Hamas? Hamas terrorists have taken advantage of the month of lull gifted to them by the West and entrenched their positions in Rafah.

On May 27th, Hamas surprised Israelis and fired a barrage of missiles toward Tel Aviv from Rafah, something they had not been able to do for the previous four months. Israel fired at Hamas targets from where the missiles were launched. That night tents in a refugee camp caught fire and over twenty civilians tragically died. It was not initially clear what caused the fire—possibly Israeli shells inadvertently hitting an oil tank, and possibly a secondary explosion of a Hamas weaponry cache. The Israel-bashing community did not wait to find out. The UN, the media, and European governments immediately demanded that Israel halt its operation against Hamas in Rafah in response. In other words, this was an open invitation for Hamas to send more missiles at Israel from Rafah, to shoot toward Israeli forces, and cause more carnage, with the international assurances that Israel would be constrained from retaliating.

Indeed, Hamas fired more missiles from Rafah to Tel Aviv on August 13th, and in what seemed to be balancing between defending the physical attack form Hamas and the ideological attack from the West, Israel did not bomb Hamas launching grounds right away. It first instructed residents of the surrounding neighborhoods to evacuate to designated safe zones, effectively alerting Hamas terrorists of the coming attack, allowing them time to evacuate along with their weapons, and even designating safe routes for them to do so. (This of course was marketed in the West as yet another episode of "ethnic cleansing.")

These events underscore how Gazan civilian casualties became the counterforce to deterrence since civilian casualties lead to international pressure on Israel to refrain from attacking Hamas, and provide for its ability to fight on. The tragic death of Gazan civilians in that fire was both ammunition for the Israel-bashers in their assault on Judaism, and a great achievement for Hamas in leveraging its second "asset"—Gazan civilians.

But the biggest leverage comes from the third "asset" at Hamas's disposal—the effective de facto drafting of Western media on which Hamas's war strategy depends, and which, as in all previous rounds, delivered for Hamas.

Draft the Western Media

Since the 2005 Israeli unilateral withdrawal from Gaza and the subsequent Hamas takeover, there have been seven big rounds of fighting with Hamas. Each carried roughly the same rhythm. First, Hamas launches rockets at Israeli civilian population centers. Israel then retaliates, hitting the missile launchers and other Hamas targets in Gaza. The Western media then portrays Israel as the aggressor, by focusing their reporting on collateral civilian casualties. In response, the international community steps in to end the Israeli counter-operations.

Maybe Hamas's holiday slogan is "We attacked Israel, Israel tried to destroy us, the media saved us, let's do it again."

Indeed, the prescribed predictable cycle depends on media intervention. Governments and international organizations require time to mobilize. Public campaigns require funding, hiring public relations firms, and plotting strategy. But the media can engage immediately!

HAMAS'S DEPENDENCY ON THE IDEOLOGICAL ASSAULT ON JUDAISM

Hamas launched the October 7th assault with the strategy of sustaining a few tough weeks or months in the tunnels, protected by human shields, and then count on their de facto partners in the media, UN, and global organizations to mount international pressure on Israel to stop its counter-operation. Israel, the thinking likely went, would eventually be forced to stop. Hence Hamas survives and can launch more attacks. Indeed, Hamas's war doctrine depends on the ideological assault on Judaism.

One can reflect with nostalgia on those days in 2005 when UN leaders, progressive activists, liberal journalists, and others, urging Israel to unilaterally withdraw from Gaza, pledged that if Israel would ever be attacked from Gaza after its withdrawal, they would all stand with Israel when it fights back against its attackers, since Israel would then have the "moral high ground."

Indeed, as discussed, following Israel's full withdrawal, which included uprooting all traces of Jewish life in Gaza, Israel enjoyed a few months of superficial love from those circles.

But when Hamas attacked Israel from Gaza, the same "moral high ground" people forgot their pledge and reverted to their addictive Israel-bashing. Seven rounds later, the "moral high ground" people are at the forefront of assaulting Judaism through Israel's protective operation in Gaza.

The Tunnel System Gives the Media Time to Work Its Magic

Hamas's October 7th attack was radically more brutal than the previous assaults it launched—but so was its preparedness. Hamas has created the "Gaza Metro"—an astonishing system of military tunnels under Gaza in which the terrorists can hide and weather the Israeli attack, be it weeks or months until the media coverage yields results and intentional pressure forces Israel to stop.

Last time, Israel was restrained after eleven days. In this round, with the tunnel system, Hamas can sustain itself for a much longer period. Those tunnels are an entire city below a city—interconnected and supplied with everything needed for a prolonged stay.

All that Hamas has to do is to sit down, relax, and let the Western media work its magic on global public opinion and then wait for public pressure to influence governments to force Israel to stop its counter-offensive. As in every other round, this worked. Within days of the October 7th massacre, demonstrations erupted in European public squares and university campuses, calling on Israel to stop its counter-operation before it even started.

Hamas was likely waiting to see what slogan its pro bono de facto partners in the West would produce. Last time it was "ethnic cleansing." This time, it was a rather simple one that effectively captured Hamas's objective.

Support for Hamas Gets a Slogan: Ceasefire Now

Hamas work is done by others—not only in public relations, media relations, and lobbying, but even in printing and product placement. Within weeks following the October 7th attack, banners, posters, stickers, social media memes, and even t-shirts appeared reading: "Ceasefire Now!"

It was an effective catch phrase: Who does not want a ceasefire? Ceasefire means no war, no shooting, and no killing. "Ceasefire Now" was not only plastered on billboards, but also appeared as the talking point for pundits, experts, TV personalities, journalists, and eventually politicians. With "Ceasefire Now," it was clear that Hamas's apparent strategy to "Draft the Media" was successful. "Ceasefire Now" means that Hamas survives, that October 7th paid off, and indeed that Hamas is all set to commit more October 7ths. Pressure soon began to be built on Israel to end its operation.

The promotion of "Ceasefire Now" was the media's de facto contribution to Hamas's physical assault on Judaism. Soon the media made an even bigger contribution to the Israel-bashers' ideological attack on Judaism.

ERADICATE JUDAISM (2024)

CHAPTER 6

MEDIA INCITES THE WORLD AGAINST THE JEWS

As discussed, Israel-bashers' path to eradicate Judaism goes through instilling a global belief that the Jewish state commits war crimes and crimes against humanity (as it has for two thousand years). They have always faced a small problem though: War crimes need a war. That gap was conveniently closed on October 7th when Hamas started a brutal one. From then on, Western media picked up the baton, using the realities of war to instill a narrative about a bad actor who kills children, slaughters babies, and murders women: the Jewish state.

In just three short months, from October 7th to the beginning of 2024, much of the world was indoctrinated with that narrative through media coverage of the war in Gaza. War naturally draws the attention of people who are otherwise not following the Israeli-Arab conflict. Since naturally such people have a limited knowledge about the conflict, those days are the most crucial to set minds. Western media is aware of this, and has done exactly that.

By November, October 7th seemed a long time ago. Now there were new alleged atrocities—those committed by Israel against the people of Gaza, and by extension, against the Palestinians. The new allegations also drew renewed attention to the narrative of Israel's occupation of the West Bank and alleged abuse of Palestinians living there.

Suddenly, the October 7th story was flipped. Israel was the aggressor and the Palestinians were cast as victims. The BBC, for example, interviewed an expert, a Palestinian educator, on October 7th, who explained to loyal BBC viewers that "an attack by Palestinian resistance is legitimate and moral. This is exactly like the Ghetto Uprising. This is the Gaza Ghetto uprising against 100 years of European and Zionist colonialism and occupation...."

Similarly, other media outlets retrofitted their narrative into a distortion of history, using "experts" that those media outlets chose based on the narrative they wanted to instill. ("It's not our fault, it is the expert's view.") Indeed, the power of the media in the first days of a conflict is so immense that it is akin to a "land grab" of unpopulated territory. If a person is unfamiliar with an issue and watches one program or reads one article, that item will dictate his views on the topic. In the days and weeks after October 7th, many news items were broadcast or written, and minds were shaped based on the Western media narrative. That shaping of minds was in tune with the Israel-bashing ideology, so deeply entrenched in Western journalists' circles...and the path to inciting the world against the Jews was paved.

A letter reportedly sent by a BBC correspondent to BBC's international staff around that time underscored the degree of such anti-Jewish incitement. In the leaked email, reported by the *Jewish Chronicle*, the BBC correspondent had encouraged the rest of the staff to use terms like "settler-colonialism" and "ethnic cleaning."

"The power of emotive coverage and repetition is well understood," the correspondent explained. "The selective application of emotive repetition is sure to have an impact on audiences."

The correspondent then went on to explain that Israel "dehumanizes Palestinians and set the stage for the mass murder they have pledged—and begun—to carry out."

This is just one example that underscores that the media is not an observer, but an active participant in the Israel-Hamas war, shaping the minds of millions around the world. This also gives a flavor to the ecosystem in which these influential journalists are a part of. To understand the process better, we need to delve into the intricacies of how the media operates, and how it has become a primary vehicle in our time for inciting the world (willingly or unwillingly) against the Jews.

JOURNALISTS AND THE CONFLICT-INDUSTRY

The city of Jerusalem includes three main constituents: Jews, Palestinians, and the "Conflict-Industry."

The Conflict-Industry is composed of Western expats living in Jerusalem. It includes those who work for the UN and its various agencies, including UNRWA, Westerns who staff European-sponsored NGOs that perpetuate the conflict, as well as diplomats representing the EU and European diplomats to the Palestinian Authority. It also includes Western journalists, who socially interact with members of the Conflict-Industry. Unlike the Jewish and Palestinian residents of Jerusalem, the Conflict-Industry is characterized by its high turnover, lavish and frequent parties, its own social hierarchy, and insularity. Indeed, the Conflict-Industry bears features that are reminiscent of European colonialism of the 20th century.

A few years ago, I attended the United Nations' Christmas party at the UN compound in Jerusalem. I was chatting with a member of the Conflict-Industry who had been in Israel for half a year. She was working with the Palestinian Authority in Ramallah and was living in a Jewish neighborhood in West Jerusalem, as do many members of the Conflict-Industry. After a few minutes of talking, she asked me where I was from. When I told her that I was from Israel, she got all excited. "I have been living here for six months," she said, "and you are only the second Israeli I have ever spoken to; the first one was my hair stylist."

This underscores the extent to which the Conflict-Industry does not interact with indigenous Israelis, nor indigenous Palestinians outside their work. They are in their own little bubble and their own echo chamber. Certainly, that echo chamber includes the frequent use of terms such as "ethnic cleansing," "genocide," "massacre," and the magic code word that must be incorporated into nearly every sentence, "occupation."

Foreign journalists in Jerusalem are socially part and parcel of the Conflict-Industry. While journalists are not homogenous and do not act in unison, many of them are friends with members of the Conflict-Industry. When an UNRWA employee holds a party, for instance, he invites his circle of Conflict-Industry friends which includes many foreign journalists. When a UN diplomat goes to have drinks at the American Colony Hotel in the Sheikh Jarrah neighborhood of East Jerusalem, he is seated next to tables full of Westerners working in European-sponsored NGOs, EU diplomats working with Palestinians, and indeed foreign journalists.

(European ambassadors to Israel live and operate in Tel Aviv since Europe does not recognize Jerusalem as part of Israel. The European diplomats in Jerusalem are diplomats that are assigned to the Palestinian Authority in Ramallah. They do not live in Ramallah, but in Jerusalem, for both security and social reasons—after all they are Westerners. Ironically, the only European country that recognizes Jerusalem as the capital of Israel and does have its embassy there is Kosovo, a European country with a Muslim majority.)

Many Western journalists' day-to-day life is closely intertwined with those in the Conflict-Industry. Therefore, they operate on the breeding grounds of anti-Jewish incitement. I am an anomaly in this group, and at times this leads to unpleasant moments. At one party, hosted by a prominent foreign journalist, I spoke to a member of the Conflict-Industry. When he learned that I served in the Israeli army, he changed his demeanor and started yelling, "Nazi! Nazi!" Pointing his finger at me while repeating, "You are a Nazi." People at the party found this late-night distraction amusing, though some perhaps were more concerned that there was enough alcohol, since the Israeli government strictly prohibits stores from selling alcohol after 11 p.m., even to foreign journalists (Occupation!).

This is the ecosystem in which at least a substantial part of Jerusalem's foreign journalist corps operates. It is nearly impossible not to be affected by it, but this environment just scratches the surface in explaining the Western media's role in inciting against the Jews and becoming an active participant in the Israel-Hamas war.

HEADLINES DRIVE PUBLIC OPINION

Journalists whose media outlet engages in distortive reporting often explain to me that "they are just following orders." It is the headquarters that dictates the coverage, they point out. To begin with, it is the editors back at headquarters who typically write headlines.

Let's take the June 16, 2017 BBC headline: "Three Palestinians killed after deadly stabbing in Jerusalem." It sounds to the casual reader, who is scanning the website, that Israel is simply "at it again" killing Palestinians.

Only deep in the story is the context unveiled: Palestinian terrorists attacked a group of Israeli police officers, killing a female officer.

A *Guardian* headline—"Israeli forces kill Palestinian after Tel Aviv shooting leaves two dead"—uses similar methods of indoctrination and incitement against Israel. This one was about a terrorist attack in Tel Aviv in April 2022, in which a Palestinian terrorist shot and killed passerbys on one of Tel Aviv's busiest streets, and then hid for hours. After a prolonged search while Tel Aviv was on de facto lockdown, the terrorist was found, and in the shoot-out with police, he was killed. Or in other words, "Israeli forces kill Palestinian after Tel Aviv shooting leaves two dead."

Headlines and slogans shape people's views. Therefore, just as it is no wonder that Europeans in the 20th century developed an innate hatred of Jews, it is no wonder that Europeans and others around the world feel the same today.

On May 15, 2018, the *New York Times*' inciting headline "Israelis kill dozens in Gaza" was accompanied by a photo of a smoke-filled field with Arabs lying on the ground, while others in the shot appeared to be trying to escape the thick black smoke—a photo perhaps reminiscent of some of the images of the Holocaust or other horrific massacres. The photo appeared "above the fold," on the top of the newspaper, and took up two-thirds of the width. One did not need to buy the *New York Times* to see the photo. It was clearly visible from a distance to anybody passing by a newsstand in New York.

Realities like this, my journalist friends assured me, had nothing to do with their work. Somebody at headquarters made that call. They merely provide the raw reporting, while the editors back at headquarters decide how to package, spin, and market that reporting.

One also has to understand the dynamic between journalists and their editors. Even if a journalist is upset about how his reporting is presented, it is doubtful how much influence he can have. Being a journalist in Jerusalem is a lucrative job. Your stories are printed more regularly than a journalist in any European city, and you are exposed to more action. It is more interesting and places you on a fast-track promotion trajectory.

Being a journalist in Jerusalem is also safe. Unlike being a journalist in other conflict areas, journalists can travel throughout Israel without security restrictions. Mostly, it is fun. Journalists are having a good time in Israel, with parties, bars, the beach, and yoga in the park. They also enjoy a sense of history, the landscape, and the culture. Journalists generally want to keep their posts in Israel. Picking a fight with supervisors because their reporting got distorted with a headline or a photo can be a risky move and threatens their post in Israel. Worse, it might paint them as someone who has "gone native," placing a cloud over their professionalism and hurting their promotion trajectory. It could trigger questions about their social contacts with indigenous Israelis, who might be planting *all sorts of ideas* in their mind.

Moreover, even if journalists are brave enough to take up the issue of inciting headlines with their editors, it would likely be a lost cause. The decision criteria at headquarters are different:

"Media is a business" journalists often explain to me. It is not just a question of political considerations or advancing the agenda of that media outlet, be it Israel-bashing, or "clandestine" campaigning for a presidential candidate. Everything is about dollars, I'm told, just as for Apple, Google, General Motors, and any other business. And Israel-bashing headlines generate clicks.

"An English Boy Dies by the River in Norwich" Is a Boring Headline

This makes sense. In the 12th century, a headline: "An English boy dies by the river in Norwich" would not generate "clicks." Sadly, at that time, children died frequently due to poor health conditions and a lack of advances in medicine. But imagine another headline: "Jews kill an English boy and use his blood to make Passover Mazos"—that generates clicks! Whether the reader believes it or is skeptical (at first), whether the reader is interested in Jews or not, such a headline would get people's attention. The same is true today.

"Hamas terrorists storm the border" is yet another routine headline. But "Jews kill Palestinians," or as the *New York Times* had it in its 2018 headline, "Israelis kill dozens in Gaza," gets the reader's attention.

I encounter this myself when editors take a headline I write and change it to drive more traffic to the story—a common practice in journalism. At times I push back. For example, a few years ago, I wrote an article with a headline that included a reference to aborting a military operation. The editors changed it to "abortion" of the operation. This is because of Search Engine Optimization (SEO) considerations. The word "abortion" drives more traffic and there will be more clicks, which in turn will lead to more ad revenues. I protested, and the editors agreed that the new headline was misleading, and changed the word back to aborting. However, to be fair to foreign journalists, while I might face some risk professionally challenging my editors, I do not face the risk of being recalled from Jerusalem, as they do. Jerusalem is my home.

Similar dynamics exist in the visual media, with the use of split screens, as well as in social media outlets of media organizations with the use of soundbites, short twits, and mind-setting photos like the one used by the *New York Times*. Indeed, the media influences minds not so much with text, but with "flags": a headline, a photo.

It is exactly what Herzl described went into the formation of German nationalism when he said, "a flag is not a stick with a rag on it.… With a flag, one can lead men wherever one wants to." Indeed, a headline and photo are not merely an introduction to an article. With a good headline and a photo, "one can lead men wherever one wants to." And sadly in our time—that destination is the assault on Judaism.

FINE PRINT: ISN'T IT TRUE THAT ISRAELIS KILLED DOZENS OF PALESTINIANS?

The agenda of much of the Western media on the day they reported "Israelis kill dozens of Palestinians" was not just about Israel. May 15, 2018, the 70th anniversary of Israel's independence in the Israeli ethos, was also the 70th anniversary of the "Nakba" in the Palestinian narrative. The Nakba—which means disaster in Arabic—marks their defeat and displacement in the 1948 war.

A day prior, President Donald Trump honored a promise he and previous presidents had made to move the American embassy to Jerusalem. Indeed, 2018 was over twenty years after the U.S. Congress passed the Jerusalem Embassy Act with an overwhelming majority of ninety-five to three in the Senate and 347 to thirty-seven in the House of Representatives. This was in 1995 when Bill Clinton was president, and he himself had pledged to move the embassy to Jerusalem.

On May 14, 2018, Trump did it.

One Democratic political operative warned me about Israelis cozying up too much to Trump by saying "If Trump kissed a Panda, I would hate Pandas." And indeed, the media used the embassy inauguration as a tool to express opposition not only to Israel but to Trump.

Early that morning, the foreign press corps gathered in a Jerusalem hotel. Many of them were on the same schedule that day, including three events. First up, a press conference with a congressional delegation which had arrived for the embassy opening ceremony scheduled for that evening, then they would head over to the Gaza border, where Hamas was planning to hold a violent Nakba day riot, then back to Jerusalem to cover the opening ceremony of the embassy.

The politicization of this once bipartisan endeavor—moving the U.S. embassy to Jerusalem—was evident in the composition of the congressional delegation, which was all Republican. Senator Ted Cruz commented: "I don't know why the Democrats will not be here, chose not to come. Every member of Congress had the option before them to come and be here. There was no way on earth we could have inaugurated this embassy without my being here to celebrate it. It's too important." Senator Lindsey Graham commented: "I would just assume that the Republicans who didn't come had [a scheduling] conflict."

As the press conference was over and reporters were ready to head to Gaza, the chat among the journalists was about what was to come: Hamas was going to try to generate many deaths, to use the attention of the embassy to get headlines, and it was going to be a mess. Hamas made it no secret. It had planned the Nakba Day events a while back and even announced a buildup that would peak with the May 15th event.

Once the U.S. announced that on May 14th it would hold an inauguration ceremony for the embassy, Hamas decided to take advantage of the media coverage and moved Nakba Day from May 15th to May 14th. Yet, the scale of the Hamas violence came as a surprise. In what now seems to have been a "dress rehearsal" for October 7, 2023, thousands of Hamas terrorists stormed the border, shooting, and firing makeshift bombs and explosive balloons towards Israel. In addition, thousands of Palestinian civilians were herded to various points around the border at the order of Hamas.

When Hamas terrorists stormed the borders, Israelis did what we can only wish they would have done on October 7, 2023: Shoot the terrorists. Indeed, dozens of Hamas terrorists died. Of all Palestinian casualties, per both Hamas and Islamic Jihad's own data, nearly all were Hamas and Islamic Jihad terrorists. The idea of reversing the "Nakba"—the disaster—by just storming the border and returning to their homes "from the river to the sea" had nothing to do with the opening of the U.S. embassy and was planned long before the embassy inauguration was announced.

Journalists knew that, but this did not stop the media from making that fake connection. Media outlets showed a split screen: Bodies on the ground in Gaza versus champagne and laughter at the American Embassy opening party in Jerusalem.

A myth was created by the media that the embassy opening had led to spontaneous riots and that Israel was shooting rioters indiscriminately. That split screen ran all day and instilled a dual false narrative, that

- The "spontaneous riots" in Gaza were a reaction to the embassy opening, e.g., innocent people died in Gaza due to Trump's recklessness.
- The Israelis celebrate while their soldiers are murdering innocent Palestinians in Gaza. Just another reaffirmation that Israelis are "happy to kill children."

If there had been split screens in 12th century England, the media would likely have shown the images of the child, William of Norwich, dead by the river, his grieving family by his body, with a split screen of Jews laughing and celebrating their Passover Seder, eating the Matzos that were presumably made from William's blood. (There were no split screens at the time, so that message was instilled through a painting centuries later, showing Jews extracting Christian children's blood.)

Western media that day doubled down on the false storyline:

"Israelis kill more than 50 Palestinians in Gaza protests, health officials say," the *Washington Post* headline read.

"Israeli forces kill dozens of Palestinians in protests as U.S. embassy opens in Jerusalem—as it happened" read the *Guardian* headline.

That evening, I saw a journalist friend who came back from Gaza. He had been working for one of the large European media outlets. I was not short of words to describe what I thought of the media distortion. "This is what the Europeans want to hear," he replied. "Europeans want to hear: Israelis kill Palestinians".

Indeed, just as "Jews kill children" is what the English public wanted to hear in the 12th century (England eventually murdered and expelled its entire Jewish community), "Israelis kill Palestinians" is what the European public wants to hear in the 21st century. (We have yet to see the consequences.) The media is merely providing a service, catering to the needs of their clients, according to that journalist.

PROVEN STRATEGY: ATTACK AND RETRACT

Indeed, Europeans, Americans, and people around the world must have felt uneasy that day, and the next morning, a Monday, when people went to work and discussed what became known as the massacre that occurred that Sunday, May 14th.

Those who would not call it a massacre were scolded. For example, Alexandria Ocasio-Cortez, then a candidate for Congress, retweeted an *Al Jazeera* tweet about the "massacre in Gaza," writing: "This is a massacre. I hope my peers have the moral courage to call it such. No state or entity is absolved of mass shootings of protesters. There is no justification. Palestinian people deserve basic human dignity, as anyone else. Democrats can't be silent about this anymore."

In the days that followed, it became evident, even to the harshest Israel-bashers, that indeed, there was no massacre. The people killed were Hamas and Islamic Jihad terrorists. Israel was correct in stopping this attack on its border. To their credit, many media outlets, including the BBC, issued a retraction.

A few weeks later, U.S. Ambassador to Israel David Friedman slammed the media coverage during a symposium held by the U.S. news agency, The MediaLine: "Where is the other case where 40,000 people rushed the border under the cover of burning tires, with Molotov cocktails, pistols and kites painted with swastikas, starting fires everywhere? Where did that happen in some other place where the people rushing the borders were committed to killing the citizens on the other side, and somebody did it better?"

Indeed, an independent study showing that Israel acted correctly was irrelevant. The headline is what counted. Friedman concluded his scolding of the media: "All you are doing is creating impressions that have no basis in fact." But facts do not matter. Mind-shaping does, and the minds were shaped here and in dozens of other instances throughout the conflict: Israel is the bad guy, Israel is committing a massacre, Israel is committing war crimes.

Who remembers the retractions?

In fact, the media strategy for a long time has been "attack and retract." For example, that 2017 BBC headline describing the murder of an Israeli policewoman as "Three Palestinians killed after deadly stabbing in Jerusalem" was later retracted, but who goes back to read old news? The "attack and retract" mind-setting strategy was successful in the "massacre in Jenin," a broad accusation that Israeli soldiers committed a massacre in 2002 against Jenin's civilian population during Israel's battle with terrorists in the West Bank city. The Jenin Massacre became a common term in left-wing circles in Europe and the U.S. The UN and others sent investigators but despite having put together a team of Israel-bashers, the commissions had to conclude the obvious: There was no massacre in Jenin. Yet this took months, and in the case of some investigations, years. In the meantime, the public was inundated with the fake news that Israel committed a massacre in Jenin. Who could possibly remember long afterwards that the ones who claimed it, also refuted it?

The same is happening in 2024 in Gaza. The media is indoctrinating the public and turning itself from a neutral bystander reporting the news to a participant in this war. Indeed, "attack and retract" has been a common media feature. Nobody remembers the retraction. The public's mind is fixed on the original false impression created through the attack.

BEING BALANCED = INCITING AGAINST THE JEWS

Another tool Western media uses to frame the world's public opinion against the Jewish state is the concept of being "balanced."

Indeed, journalists say that much of the criticism leveled at them is unjustified, because they present both sides. The reader can form his own views. We bring both sides for his consideration. But certain things are not balanced. Reporting a murder in a school cannot be reported in a balanced way, and neither can October 7th and the Hamas versus Israel war. The difference is that a school murderer does not issue a press release, give the media talking points, or have a pro bono public relations firm operating behind him. But Hamas does, and a journalist is trained to cut and paste from each of the side's press releases, to use each side's talking points, and describe the resulting news story as "balanced."

Moreover, in Gaza, reporters say that they got their information from "health officials"—often ignoring that it is Hamas who controls the Ministry of Health along with the rest of Gaza's government agencies. Therefore, a story pits the word of the (colonialist) Israeli army against (credible) Gaza Health officials.

If the media reports the Gaza War in a balanced way, does this mean it reports other events in a balanced way? Was 9/11 reported in a balanced way? Was equal space given to both sides? Or was there a "media bias" toward the American side?

The other side had its own narrative as well: McDonald's restaurants were opening in Saudi Arabia; there was an attempt to Americanize the conservative Muslim population; Americans had too much influence over culture in the Middle East; and Islam was under threat. How many interviews were there with Osama Bin Laden or someone speaking on his behalf on CNN, BBC and other leading media organizations? How many Al Qaeda talking points were read? None and appropriately so.

The same should apply to Israel's 9/11 and the Gaza War. Reporting the Hamas narrative is technically being balanced, but just as reporting 9/11 would have amounted to a secondary verbal assault on America, reporting the Hamas side is part of the assault on Judaism.

The same can be said about the Holocaust. There are frequent programs and articles done about the Holocaust today. Is it reported in a "balanced way" as required by journalistic integrity? There was a narrative on the other side: The Jews were taking over Europe, dehumanizing Europeans, polluting humanity, controlling the media, and controlling the banking system. If there is space given to those accusations, it is in explaining how the Europeans were incited against the Jews, not in the context of factual reporting such as, "according to (credible) German health officials, Jews have been polluting the water supply, as part of the Jewish attempt to take over Europe through starvation of the European population."

Did balanced reporting contribute to the massacre and expulsion of Jews from England in the aftermath of the William of Norwich "incident"? "English officials argue that Jews killed him and used his blood for Passover Matzos; Jews deny it." There you go: balanced reporting!

None of the history programs about previous assaults on Judaism are reported in a "balanced way"—programs about the Holocaust, William of Norwich, the Spanish deportation of

Jews, the French expulsion of Jews. But news and analysis of the current assault on Judaism is reported in a balanced way. Why is that? One of the reasons is the broadly accepted American stance of having zero tolerance for traditional antisemitism (the existential threat to Judaism of the last century), and a green light for Israel-bashing and anti-Zionism (the existential threat to Judaism in this century).

There would be public outcry if a media outlet read talking points from Hitler's *Mein Kampf* as a way to present the Nazi rationale in its conflict with European Jewry. The producer and journalists would be fired, and rightly so. Meanwhile, in today's Gaza War, media outlets read Hamas's talking points and that is tolerated, not just tolerated but held up as an example of "balanced reporting."

And this is exactly the backdrop to the event that shaped the minds of many of the "swing voters" in world public opinion concerning the Gaza war.

IT ALL COMES NICELY TOGETHER: ISRAEL BOMBS A HOSPITAL IN GAZA

On October 17, 2023, an explosion occurred in the Al-Ahli Arab Hospital in Gaza, leading to dozens of Palestinian deaths. The Western media knew early on that the deaths were likely caused by an Islamic Jihad rocket fired from the Gaza Strip, intended for Israel, which fell way short of its target and landed on this Gazan hospital, but they did not report it as such.

The Israeli army was quick to show evidence to journalists. Within a few hours, Israeli media aired footage of a rocket coming from Gaza landing in the vicinity of the hospital. The western media also knew that a large number of rockets that are fired at

Israel by Hamas and Islamic Jihad land in Gaza, leading to heavy Palestinian casualties. It was estimated at the time that as many as a third of their rockets land in Gaza, and that a significant portion of Palestinian civilian casualties are caused by these errant Hamas rockets.

The journalists also knew that Israel does not bomb hospitals deliberately and a mistake like this was highly unlikely. From the get-go, journalists knew. And still…this was the headline on the BBC's website that evening: "Hundreds killed in Israeli strike on Gaza hospital—Palestine officials." Similar headlines and reporting appeared in TV news coverage and throughout the gamut of Western media. Ten days after October 7th, millions of people around the world, who by now were confused about who was the villain in the conflict, were then certain: The Jews bombed a hospital!

It is one thing to kill a child for his blood, but to target an entire hospital, where people are sick, where women deliver babies, and then kill hundreds in that hospital?

Now the "balanced reporting" about Jews starting World War I, as reported in that ("credible") German book *Mein Kampf*, is beginning to make sense. That reporting was also prevalent in German and European media through the 1920s and 1930s, and set global mindset.

"Israeli Strike Kills Hundreds in Hospital, Palestinians Say," read the *New York Times* headline, alongside photos of grieving victims in the hospital.

"Hundreds killed in Israel strike on Gaza hospital, officials say," read the CNN headline.

CNN took it one step further than the BBC. The BBC pulled out the "balanced reporting" weapon by saying that this report, if anybody paid attention to the last words of the headline, separated by a hyphen, was issued by *Palestinian* officials.

CNN did not bother to mention that. The network did qualify that the claim of "hundreds killed in Israel strike" was according to officials. But who were those officials? American officials? Israeli officials? Certainly credible people, because they are "officials." There was no mention that these were officials of the Hamas terrorist organization. Imagine a headline: "The U.S. invented 9/11, officials say," not mentioning that these were Al Qaeda officials.

The *Los Angeles Times* interrupted Californians' peaceful lives with the headline, "At least 500 killed in Israeli airstrike on Gaza City hospital, Gaza Health Ministry says."

Now the officials are known; they are the credible Gaza Health Ministry. But the casual reader has no way of knowing that the Gaza Health Ministry is an outlet of Hamas. To be fair, the body of most articles specified that the source was Palestinian officials and that Israelis were investigating or denying. But as discussed above, minds are made up by headlines.

Western journalists point out that at least they were not reporting as Al Jazeera, whose headline read: "Hundreds of casualties as Israel hits Gaza hospital sheltering thousands."

As in Jenin in 2002, as in Hamas's attempted invasion of Israel in 2018 during the U.S. embassy opening, as with dozens of other terrorist attacks against Israel, the media shaped people's minds with its initial reporting, turning foul into fair and fair into foul, and nobody was there to notice the retraction.

All the elements that go into the media incitement were present in the Western media coverage of the hospital bombing: The "balanced reporting," the journalists being embedded with the Conflict-Industry, who naturally parroted Hamas talking points, the agenda of the news organizations, and the use of headlines to shape public opinion.

And certainly, the good old strategy of "attack and retract." After the poison was spread and millions around the world understood the degree of Israel's cruelty, which perhaps justified the October 7th attack to begin with, there was the little-noticed retraction. Within a few days, all media outlets acknowledged that they were wrong—it had been an Islamic Jihad rocket.

On the evening of the attack, the IDF spokesperson held a press conference. In a somewhat unusual move, he used the press conference to scold the journalists for their network's coverage.

And still, the journalists in the room refused to believe the truth that they were aware of. In a show of just how deeply rooted the assault on Judaism is, journalists ignored facts, overruled their own judgment, and sidestepped their own knowledge.

One journalist, from CNN, said what other journalists likely felt. After asking the spokesperson a clarifying question and hearing the evidence that Israel did not do it—that it was an Islamic Jihad missile, the journalist scolded the military spokesperson: "Why should we believe you?"

Despite facts, data, and even declassified material that compromised Israel's intelligence assets and were shared with the journalists, many of the journalists, refused to let go of the headline: "Hundreds killed in Israel strike on Gaza hospital."

They refused to believe anything else. This just shows how right Herzl was when he said that dogmatic minds cannot be changed: Stop trying to convince Europeans that the Jews do not poison the wells or are not taking over Europe. It won't work. Instead, start thinking of a paradigm shift (see Chapter 11).

But it is not only the dogmatic minds of journalists that cannot be changed. Soon there was a bigger "why should we believe you?" A question started to percolate through the fringes of Europe and progressive U.S. society, making its way to the mainstream: Did Israel invent October 7th? Did Israel make up that story so they could, to use the words of that BBC correspondent, "set the stage for the mass murder they have pledged—and begun—to carry out"?

Was October 7th a "false flag"—a Jewish ploy, so Jews could carry out their genocide of Palestinians, just as they planned the genocide of Europeans in the early 20th century (which "thankfully" was stopped due to actions by the German government)? More and more believe that. According to CyberWell, October 7th denial posts on social media were viewed by more than 15 million people around the world by March 2024.

"Why should we believe you"? became bigger and bigger—why should we believe you Jews that the Holocaust happened? Why should we believe you Jews when you claim you do not use Christian children's blood in your recipe for Passover Matzos? Why should we believe you Jews when you claim you did not poison the wells of Europe; when you claim you did not try to use starvation as a tool in your attempted genocide of the European population? Why should we believe you?

The media has long been accused of drawing a moral equivalence between the actions of Hamas and those of Israel. But in reporting the hospital bombing, it was no longer using moral equivalence—it was choosing Hamas "morality"—the lie that Israel bombed the hospital, as more credible than the Israeli denial.

One can dress up the media participation in the 21st century assault on Judaism in whatever euphemism one chooses: "Balanced reporting" or "Moral equivalence," but one cannot ignore that the 21st century global mindset about the Jews was set by Western media.

MEDIA AS AN ACTOR IN THE WAR

Even after it was crystal clear that Western media's reporting was wrong, even after Hamas itself conceded it was not Israel, but Islamic Jihad, it was hard for the media outlets to let go.

Even after the BBC acknowledged that millions of their viewers and web readers were fed the wrong information, they still insisted that they were not at fault—and that was due to the "balanced reporting pagan." They issued a statement: "We reject these claims about our coverage; anyone watching, listening to, or reading it can see we have set out both sides' competing claims about the attack."

There we have it: Jews got together to create World War I, leading to millions of European deaths, according to (credible) German officials, who added that if Jews are not stopped, they will do it again, leading to more European deaths.... On the other side, it should be noted that (sleazy, lying) Jews deny they did it."—per the BBC statement, this would be a fine example of balanced reporting!

Let's say it clearly: "Balanced reporting" is a tool in the Israel-basher's assault on Judaism. Indeed, the media reporting of the Gaza War can serve as a case study for scholars studying the Holocaust and other historical events. It is a great tool for understanding the past and human behavior.

We don't need a war to do that; we can just read Theodor Herzl, who predicted such patterns. As a journalist, he understood the power of his pen. There he was, sitting in the press balcony of the French Parliament in the 1890s, writing for the leading European newspaper *Neue Freie Presse*, about French politics.

People's views of France were shaped by his opinions—and he, unlike today's journalists, made no secret that he was writing his own opinions. So much so, that the French security forces spied on him. They understood his power as a journalist, and that his, and the writing of other journalists, was a matter of French National Security. And they treated it that way.

Today too, as seen in the media coverage of the Gaza War, the reporting is a matter of global security (though thankfully it is not treated the way France treated it in the 1890s, thanks to the freedom of the press and freedom of speech). Herzl understood how easy it is to change people's minds and he applied that knowledge to his understanding of European incitement against the Jews.

He studied the endeavors of Bismarck, who built a German empire out of autonomous principalities. Herzl realized how simple it was: "What went into the making of the German Empire? Dreams, songs, fantasies, and black-red-and-gold ribbons—and in short order. Bismarck merely shook the tree which the visionaries had planted."

Herzl also saw how easy it is to incite the majority of the French public in the aftermath of the Dreyfus affairs. The public knew by then that the Jewish officer was framed (by the same national security unit that spied on Herzl), but refused to let go of the headline: "Dreyfus is a traitor," which served as a valuable indication that Jews are traitors, that Jews are sleazy, and that Jews corrupt France.

In 1929, a journalist came to interview the elder former French Prime Minster Georges Clemenceau about his memories of Herzl. It had been over thirty-five years since Herzl's Paris days when he rubbed elbows with the French political, social, and intellectual elite, including Clemenceau. For four years,

Herzl carefully studied the intricacies of the French democracy—its strengths and its flaws—and applied his observations in envisioning a more perfect European liberal democracy in the Jewish state.

Clemenceau offered his thoughts not only about Herzl but also about how journalism evolved since the days of Herzl, who died in 1904.

Clemenceau led France in World War I, and along with U.S. President Woodrow Wilson and British Prime Minister David Lloyd George, presided over the 1919 Paris Peace Conference that still governs much of the world order today. He was known as "The Tiger" and was not shy about speaking his mind.

He scolded the journalist about how journalism had changed since Herzl's time. Journalists used to voice their own opinions; now they pretend to just report "facts," which are really just "writing down those [opinions] of others," the Tiger reflected.

Journalism was not designed to be "neutral," but today it wears a mask of neutrality. When French author Alexandre Dumas wanted to chime in on debate between monarchy and republicanism, the defining issue of the 19th century, he did so by writing a novel, *The Three Musketeers*. Now when a journalist wants to chime in on an issue of the day, he writes a "balanced" article. (Dumas also offered his views on the topic of Jews returning to their ancestral homeland.)

When Western media reported 9/11, it did not apply the "balance reporting" concept, and rightfully so. It did not give any credibility to the "not happened in a vacuum" aspect of the Al Qaeda narrative. It reported from the standpoint of its Western values and morality. But when it comes to the Hamas versus Israel war, journalism pretends to be "neutral" on those values, and reports the events, in a "balanced way."

Journalism coverage of the Gaza War came under more criticism when HonestReporting revealed that Gaza-based journalists might have been "embedded" in the Hamas October 7th raid. Then, on June 9, 2024, the day after the Israeli army rescued four hostages from Gaza, the Israeli Defense Forces spokesperson confirmed that three of the hostages were held by a Gaza journalist who worked for Al Jazeera and other outlets.

This of course should not reflect on journalists in general, but what is interesting is that the same journalist-terrorist also held a position in the Hamas government as a spokesperson in one of its ministries—a "Gaza official" providing balance to the Western media.

We have come full circle. The Western media claims to be balanced based on "Gaza officials" and at least one such official is a terrorist holding Israeli hostages. We can now revise the BBC statement rejecting bias in the hospital explosion to read, "We have set out both side's competing claims about the attack"—kidnapper and hostage.

The "journalist" was killed in the rescue operation, and of course Western media reported this too in a "balanced way." The *New York Times* headline read: "Israel rescues 4 hostages; Gaza officials say scores of Palestinians are killed."

The media did not stop there. Even when reporting that the hostages were held by a journalist, CNN could not help but invoke the "Why should we believe you" principle when it comes to the Jewish state. It reported on June 10th: "Israel alleges journalist held hostages in Gaza, without providing evidence."

The ideological assault on Judaism has spread so broadly that it impacts even audiences who consume news on unrelated matters: In the June 27, 2024 presidential debate between Donald Trump and Joe Biden, CNN moderate Dana Bash, who is a highly regarded journalist and considered by many as fair when it comes to Israel, asked Trump: "Would you support the creation of an independent Palestinian state in order to achieve peace in the region?" For the forty-eight million viewers, most of them not following closely the history of the Middle East, it seems from the question that it is Israel who is standing in the way of peace by denying the establishment of "an independent Palestinian state"—something that is detached from both reality on the ground and historical context.

This would be akin to asking President Bush in 2005, "Would you support Israel's unilateral withdrawal from Gaza in order to achieve peace in the region?" The answer was then yes, the direct result: October 7th, as well as years of Hamas firing missiles and rockets at Israel.

This would also be similar to asking President Clinton in 2000: "Would you support Israel's unilateral withdrawal from Lebanon in order to achieve peace in the region?" The answer was then yes, the direct result: today's atrocious attack by Hezbollah resulting in dozens of Israeli casualties, including 12 children in one attack on July 27, 2023, as well as evacuation of Israel's northern communities. This was followed by years of conflict, including the 2006 Lebanon war—all starting with the unilateral withdrawal of Israeli to "achieve peace in the region," to use Bash's words. How could unsuspecting audiences watching a debate know that in the question itself lies some subtle Israel-bashing propaganda?

The ideological assault on Judaism is unfolding before our eyes. It is nuanced, sophisticated, and elegant.

We saw similar dynamics with the ideological assault that governed the last attempt to eradicate Judaism. Indeed, Herzl understood how nuanced the ideological attack on Judaism was in his time, then conducted through the ideology of antisemitism, just as it is now conducted through the ideology of Israel-bashing: "In Paris, then, I gained a more liberal attitude toward antisemitism which I now began to understand historically and make allowances for," he wrote in 1895.

Antisemitism was not just manifested in vocal anti-Jewish slogans, it was layered and filtered through the interaction of day-to-day society, in parties, in cafes, in casual conversations, as Herzl earlier wrote: "Till recently antisemitism in France has been something comfortable and polite, one can even say pleasant."

And yet that polite, pleasant ideology of antisemitism served as the bedrock of the Nazis's attempt to eradicate Judaism just a few decades later. The same is true today with the Israel-bashing ideology. It has served as the bedrock ideology to eradicate Judaism.

The events of 2024 showed just how the media is using "acceptable" tools, such as balanced reporting, the choice of headlines, the tactic of "attack and retract," misleading questions, as well as the biased social environment of the journalist, to incite the world against the Jewish state. The Western media has fulfilled its role, the public is incited, and now it is time for the next phase in the path to eradication of Judaism.

Indeed, having an incited public is still by itself not necessarily an immediate threat to the survival of Judaism. For that to happen, governments need to step in. And that is exactly what happened in early 2024.

CHAPTER 7

GOVERNMENTS JOIN THE ASSAULT

The media incitement was effective. It shaped public opinion against Israel, and once again global anger towards the Jews was fermenting. Jews around the world suddenly felt a global finger pointed at them. A threatening finger that blamed them for committing the worst crimes against the human race.

And yet, we are not in the 1940s. Jews in the United States, Canada, France, and the United Kingdom felt safe in 2024, since they knew their governments would protect them. Governments are there to protect groups in their country that feel threatened, that are targeted and then attacked. Jews therefore should be assured that unlike in the 20th century assault on Judaism, if such a large-scale assault occurred today, the United States, Canada, and Europe will all be there to save them, individually and collectively. Governments will not tolerate an assault on the Jews, and would certainly not tolerate an assault on Judaism. In fact, this was one of the most common pushbacks I got over the years to my argument that we are in the midst of a large-scale assault on Judaism funneled through the port of Zionism.

In my articles and *Judaism 3.0* book, I underscored that Judaism is under an existential threat. I also expressed this in the deliberations of the Judaism 3.0 think tank, including on that September 13th event, merely three weeks before the October 7th attack. The criticism was in two layers. Some did not view the threat to be half as ominous as I described it. Others argued that even if I was correct and we were looking at an incoming large-scale assault on Judaism that would include sanctions, arrest warrants, and boycotts, foreign governments would be there to protect Israel and protect the Jews. Therefore, my arguments, as one critic argued, are suited for a different era—not an era where the Jews and Israel enjoy global support. This was also the pushback Theodor Herzl received when he rang the alarm bells in the late 1890s. Many thought he was exaggerating the threat to Judaism stemming from the growing antisemitism movement, but even those who shared his concerns argued that it was not consequential. Governments will be there to protect the Jews.

Indeed, rulers of European powers at the end of the 19th century, some more friendly to Jews than others, would not lend a hand to mass violence against the Jews. Yet, Herzl argued back that at the end of the day governments are subject to the will of the people. Today they are friendly, he argued, but what if one day they faced massive public pressure against the Jews?

This was especially the case with democracies. For four years, Herzl studied the nuances of French politics from the press balcony of the French Parliament. He understood just how vulnerable politicians are to the perceived sentiments of the people. Herzl understood that the country's leaders were concerned with getting elected, not with protecting the Jews. As long as those were in tandem, then indeed they would protect the Jews. In other words, as long as protecting the Jews is perceived to be in line with the will of the people, the leaders will do that, and Jews will be safe. But if the populace turned against the Jews, governments would not be able to save them.

But this was not only the case in democracies, Herzl argued. He stressed that dictatorships and monarchies are also subjected to public sentiment. Even if world leaders wanted to support the Jews, he argues, they cannot protect us: "They would only feel popular hatred by showing us too much favor."

Indeed, in the weeks after October 7th, world governments were with the Jews. U.S. Secretary of State Antony Blinken flew to Israel and stated that America will always be with Israel: "You may be strong enough on your own to defend yourself. But as long as America exists, you will never ever have to. We will always be there by your side." Canadian Prime Minister Justin Trudeau issued a statement on October 8th: "To our Israeli friends, Canadians stand with you. The Government of Canada stands ready to support you—our support for the Israeli people is steadfast." This was before the media turned the hearts of the people against Israel.

In the following weeks, as Western media outlets engaged in large-scale incitement against the Jewish state, that incitement, just as Herzl predicted, soon trickled up to once pro-Jewish governments.

TRUDEAU HAS DINNER

On November 14, 2023, the Canadian prime minister enjoyed a dinner at a Vancouver restaurant. Others were unhappy about him being there and began chanting the slogan they had been hearing in the media for weeks: "Ceasefire now, Ceasefire now."

As protesters gathered outside the restaurant waving Palestinian flags, and as the yelling of protesters inside the restaurant became louder and louder, Trudeau was escorted out of the restaurant by his security detail.

This, just as Herzl predicted, had an effect—an immediate effect.

The following day, on November 15th, Trudeau called a news conference. Once on stage, it was clear he was reversing by 180 degrees his previous support for the Jewish state, and for its war on Hamas. He urged Israel to stop "this killing of women, of children, of babies."

A little tickle and the leader—for whom Jews are near to his heart—turned. Trudeau switched from "our *support* for the Israeli people is steadfast" to our *opposition* to the Israeli people is steadfast—you are killing women, children, and babies. In doing so, Trudeau gave an enormous boost of credibility to Israel-bashers and those assaulting Judaism. Media that was previously accused of bias against Israel got official validation. This was the prime minister of Canada, who is in the know, who gets security briefings, and views himself as pro-Israel. He made it official. If there was still public opinion someplace around the world that was skeptical that Jews in Israel are (once again) committing atrocities against humanity, now there was no doubt— they are killing women, children, and babies (as they have done for two thousand years).

Trudeau made no secret of why he turned on the Jews so quickly. He stated it openly: "The world is watching, on TV, on social media—we're hearing the testimonies of doctors, family members, survivors, and kids who have lost their parents." By certifying what Israel-bashing has been saying for years, Trudeau strengthened the path to destruction of Judaism. The media sets public opinions, and those public opinions set the positions of governments. Now all that was left to do was for governments to act against the Jews—it's deja vu all over again.

The media is the one choosing to show on TV those "testimonies of doctors, family members, survivors, and kids who have lost their parents." This is the same media that chose not to show such "testimonies" when it came to the U.S. war in Afghanistan and in Iraq, not to mention when the Allies attacked Germany in World War II.

Trudeau needs to be understood. He does not control the media. Once millions of people are exposed to those horrific images, Trudeau, just as Herzl predicted, had to switch sides, as he "would only feel popular hatred by showing us too much favor." At the time, Trudeau's statement seemed outrageous. But soon outrageous became the "new normal," as the ideological assault against Judaism continued to escalate. Trudeau's switch in rhetoric was echoed by European leaders, but soon, an escalation in the ideological assault on Judaism came from an unexpected direction—the floor of the U.S. Senate.

SCHUMER MAKES A SPEECH

"A pariah opposed by the rest of the world"—this was not a quote of Haman in the Book of Esther when he made his pitch to eradicate Judaism. Nor is it a quote from the Nazis as they rationalized their efforts to kill Jews and destroy Judaism. This is a description of the Jewish state in 2024, as per U.S. Senator Chuck Schumer.

Schumer went on to imply that Jews in Israel are bigots, defining bigots as "those who oppose the idea of a Palestinian state," which today are the vast majority of Israeli Jews on the Left and Right alike. But Schumer, a strong supporter of Israel for decades, accompanied those harsh words with a friendly advice:

"Stop being that pariah." He even offered a path for Israel to doing that—recognize a state of Palestine, call for elections, fire the prime minister, and go back to Oslo—the 1993 agreement which marked the beginning of the Israeli-Palestinian conflict as we know it today, leading to over one thousand Jewish deaths during the Intifada that followed, as well as to the birth of the "Conflict-Industry."

Schumer did not mention suicide in his advice on how to stop being that pariah, but if his forty-five-minute speech had been any longer…. After all, if Judaism committed suicide and ceased to exist, the people who were formally Jews would be liberated from the hate that is directed at them, right? Herzl had an answer for that too—they will be hated as "former Jews." If enough Jews converted, the term would change from "Jewish pig" to "baptized pig," Herzl predicted.

Indeed, Schumer stopped short of suicide in his friendly advice to the Jewish state.

The Alarm Bell in Schumer's Speech

Schumer's assault had far more significance than Trudeau's and European leaders' assaults. Schumer is a mainstream U.S. senator, a Jew, and a long-time supporter of Israel. So much so that he likes to tell his Jewish donors that his last name is "Shomer," which means guardian in Hebrew and that his role in life is to be "Shomer Israel," a guardian of Israel.

This has two implications. Here we have a guardian of Israel "confessing" that the problem is indeed with Israel. He certifies that the Jewish state is indeed a pariah and its Jewish citizens are indeed bigots. This is no longer a view by some fringe Israel-bashing radical, this is no longer a view of a journalist echoing the sentiment in the Conflict-Industry—this is a guardian of Israel who certifies that the accusations leveled at Israel are indeed correct.

More alarmingly is that Schumer is an astute politician. He was first elected to office in 1974! For anybody to survive half a century in U.S. politics and achieve those impressive mile-stones—including being the leader of the Senate—one must be a very good reader of the public sentiment. Schumer certainly is.

For Schumer to make a legacy-changing decision after fifty years, from being the Guardian of Israel, to being the person Israelis will remember as the senator who attacked Israel in its hour of need is telling. This no doubt reflects Schumer's read of the shift in public sentiments. Applying Herzl's framework that leaders are subject to the populace's sentiments, we can learn from Schumer's actions the sharp degree of change in public sentiment. If there was any hope that Schumer's speech was an anomaly, those hopes were dashed when a few days later President Biden came out in support of Schumer and even dis-closed that Schumer had coordinated the speech with him.

By early 2024, it was clear that Judaism is no longer under assault by fringe individuals or members of the Conflict-Industry. We were in the midst of a large-scale assault on Judaism that is coming from the centers of power. "In every generation, some-one rises up to eradicate us," and by early 2024, it was clear that the illusion of September 2013—that this generation is differ-ent—was shattered.

The path to destruction of Judaism, outlined in that Judaism 3.0 September event, was well on its way. Hamas's attack has trig-gered large-scale incitements against the Jews. This has led to public pressure on governments, even those most friendly to the Jewish state, and those governments have turned. The rhet-oric coming from those governments was alarming, but just as in the 20th century attempt to eradicate Judaism, soon that rhetoric turned into action. The destruction mechanisms have been activated.

CHAPTER 8

DESTRUCTION MECHANISMS ACTIVATED

As discussed in previous chapters, different assaults on Judaism used different mechanisms to eliminate Jews. Sometimes it was through collective elimination, targeting the idea of Judaism, such as in 16th century Spain, and sometimes it was through killing Jew-by-Jew as in 20th century Europe.

The 2023–2024 assault is misunderstood. The focus is naturally on the October 7th physical attack by Hamas that sought to kill Jew-by-Jew, but the destruction mechanisms of Judaism are housed and controlled by the West—by Israel's allies—and the path to destruction is through collective elimination—ending the idea of Judaism. It is true that Hamas makes it no secret that it wants to kill all Jews, and on one day, on October 7th, it succeeded in killing twelve hundred Jews, using cruelty reminiscent of the Nazis' attempt to kill Jew-by-Jew: burning people alive, raping, gassing people in their own homes, beheading, and kidnapping. The Jew-by-Jew killing was complemented by terrorism originating in the West Bank, by rockets and missiles fired from Lebanon by Hezbollah, and on April 13th, by over two hundred missiles and drones fired from Iran that could have killed thousands of Jews had they not been miraculously intercepted by Israeli air defense systems and allies' fighter jets. Those efforts continued in the summer of 2024 from Iran and its proxies, trying to kill as many Jews as they can.

And still, neither Iran, Hamas, Hezbollah, nor the Houthis have the capabilities to eradicate Judaism. But the West does.

The prelude to activating those mechanisms lasted for a few months, throughout the fall of 2023. As described in previous chapters, it centered around the incitement by the media against the Jewish state, which led to setting global opinion, creating public pressure on governments, and eventually harsh rhetoric by those once pro-Jewish governments.

During the Holocaust, Germany's destruction mechanisms were not activated right away either. There was a long "prelude" at first. The Wannsee Conference, where the Final Solution was decided and the process to eradicate Judaism by killing Jew-by-Jew was launched, happened a full nine years after Hitler became Chancellor of Germany and the Nazis took control of the German government. It also occurred over three years after Kristallnacht, where Jews were attacked in riots throughout Germany and Austria.

Indeed, going into the holiday season ending 2023, the concept of sanctions against the victims of the Hamas attack seemed far-fetched, the idea of arrests of Israelis delusional, and the thought of turning Israel into the pariah, outright paranoid. As 2024 began, this all changed. The escalation came from an unexpected place: The United States of America.

FROM RHETORIC TO ACTIONS: SANCTIONS BY THE UNITED STATES…BUT ONLY AGAINST CRIMINALS

In November 2023, three Arab students were shot in Vermont, in what was believed to be a hate crime. A month later, a man in Illinois attacked an Arab woman and her six-year-old child with a knife, murdering the child—again, a hate crime.

American media covered broadly the rise of anti-Arab violence in the United States, a phenomenon that had been going on for years. The University of California at Berkeley and the Council on American–Islamic Relations claimed that anti-Arab violence in the United States is deep-rooted. They identified thirty-three groups, who received $206 million worth of funding over five years, "to promote prejudice against, or hatred of, Islam and Muslims."

Similarly in Europe, various organizations have been reporting a sharp rise in anti-Arab violence over the last decade. For example, in December 2023, EU's High Representative for Foreign Affairs and Security Policy Josep Borrell warned about the historic proportions of European anti-Muslim violence: "Tragically, history repeats itself. Conflicts and disinformation worldwide are sowing the seeds of hatred.… We cannot make the same mistakes of the past."

Indeed, anti-Arab violence rose sharply around the world. Violent incidents in Israel and the West Bank, condemnable as they are, are isolated and handled harshly not just by the Israeli police, but also by a special unit of the General Security Service, called "the Jewish Department."

Nevertheless, youths on the fringe of Israeli society have engaged in deplorable violence against Palestinians on a regular basis including vandalism, stone-throwing, and physical attacks.

Like any other society, Israel also has troubled youths as well as criminals. While not as widespread as anti-Arab violence, rhetoric, and culture in Europe and the United States, Israelis on the Left and Right agree that Israel must hold itself to higher standards, and therefore such violence is handled harshly.

This, in turn, has drawn criticism of over-enforcement, such as in the events leading to the tragic death of Ahuvia Sandak, a Jewish teenager killed in a car accident as he was being chased by undercover police detectives suspecting him of planning to throw stones at Arabs. And yet, with all the anti-Arab violence around the world, the United States decided to single out Israel and did so in a dramatic way.

On February 1, 2024, President Biden issued an executive order sanctioning four Israeli individuals, who were arrested or investigated by Israeli authorities for suspected crimes ranging from throwing stones to setting stores on fire in West Bank villages. How could the Biden administration justify that in reaction to the October 7th massacre, it would single out Israel and issue unprecedented sanctions against Israeli perpetrators, as opposed to against French or Americans, where anti-Arab violence is much more prevalent?

The administration was prepared for that question, and in the executive order itself clarified that unlike violence in other places, the violence by those Israelis "undermines the foreign policy objectives of the United States, including the viability of a two-state solution."

Shooting Arabs in Vermont does not undermine the viability of the two-state solution. Similarly, the murder of an Arab child in Chicago does not undermine the viability of the two-state solution. But stone-throwing and vandalism by four Israeli thugs apparently does. Moreover, since the overwhelming majority of

Israelis, on Right and Left alike, are opposed to the two-state solution, the Biden administration seems to have used the executive order as an opening for the theoretical sanctions against the majority of Israelis—those heretics who "undermine the foreign policy objectives of the United States" of the two-state solution.

Through the February 1, 2024 sanctions, the Biden administration accomplished much more than punishing four individuals on the fringe of Israeli society: It planted the fable that there is large-scale violence against Palestinians by the settler population.

It opened the door for more sanctions against a broader set of Israeli Jews, by more actors.

That door was opened not just from a signaling point of view, but also from a practical point of view. The executive order gave officials in the U.S. Treasury and State Departments a "license to sanction" more Israeli Jews. Indeed, on April 19th, the U.S. Treasury Department sanctioned Israeli organizations that dared raise money for the defense of individuals sanctioned in the first round of sanctions, arguing that "such acts by these organizations undermine the peace, security, and stability of the West Bank." More sanctions soon followed. The executive order was not only "the gift that keeps on giving" to those wishing to sanction Israeli Jews, but it also lowered the threshold to impose sanctions going forward to include opposing the political objectives of the administration, controversial as they might be.

No doubt, President Biden set an incredibly low bar for a future president to sanction foreign individuals who disagree with his foreign policy objective. Can one imagine President Trump imposing sanctions on European individuals who "undermine the foreign policy objective of the United States," including the recognition of Jerusalem as the capital of Israel?

Furthermore, can one imagine sanctions against those who "undermine the foreign policy objective of the United States," including the rejection of a two-state solution? After all, the two-state solution is a relic of the 1990s, rejected by Israelis, Palestinians, and experts (including Henry Kissinger, shortly before his death). It is completely possible that a future president could view the repudiation of that outdated Western idea as a foreign policy objective. Indeed, Trump expressed his skepticism about the two-state solution in an interview with *Time* magazine on April 30, 2024.

Moreover, Biden provided a "kosher certificate" for others who wish to sanction the Jewish state and its residents, a dream come true for Israel-bashers. Biden administration officials and proponents can assure Israel that they will not sanction "all Israelis who oppose the two-state solution." It is clear to even Biden's harshest critics that he would not engage in such ludicrous behavior. Yet, in issuing this first round of sanctions, Biden has shifted power, not only from the White House to government agencies, but also from America to others around the world. It gave a de facto green light to others to sanction Israel and Israeli Jews.

Biden's sanctions, received with open enthusiasm by Israel-bashers, means it is "open season" on Israeli Jews—and that was understood right away by those who have been sanctioning Jews for centuries.

EUROPEANS JOINING SANCTIONS AND EXPANDING THE JEWS TARGETED

Century after century, Europeans have been imposing sanctions against Jews—sometimes individually, sometimes collectively.

Oftentimes, those sanctions were masked as against only a subset of Jews, against individuals who happened to be Jewish, or against surrogates that everybody understood really meant the Jews.

For example, in the 17th century, France issued sanctions against Jews through the "Office of Beggars and Jews." There were too many beggars in the streets—it was "intolerable," and it was time to handle the problem by taking strong action. At various times, European sanctions targeted different aspects of Jewish life. Limits were placed on where Jews could live, for instance, or how many (if any) children Jews were allowed to have, and throughout European history, which professions Jews could work in.

Inappropriate Jewish behavior was "punished" by more sanctions. Even if the sanctions targeted a different subset of Jews or even individual Jews, the message of a new set of European sanctions came in loud and clear: Jews were placed on notice.

For two thousand years, sanctions were a primary tool through which Europe conducted its relationship with its Jewish population, and instilled Jewish insecurity.

Snub of the American Revolution

The American Revolution was a rebellion against old European dogmas, including the well-instilled European notion that when things are good, you thank the monarch, and when things are bad, you blame the Jews. America created a principle that went against the core of Europeanism: "All men are created equal." This included Jews. Therefore, the American Revolution was a negation of the European use of sanctions against Jews. In America, Jews could live wherever they chose, they could work in whichever profession they liked and were no longer limited by the number of children they could have.

It is easy to downplay the February 2024 American sanctions as merely against four thugs who engaged in despicable criminal activities, but imposing those sanctions, as well as the rounds of sanctions that soon followed, represent a reversal from the principles of the American Revolution.

Moreover, by initiating rounds of sanctions against Israeli Jews, the Biden administration provided a clear green light to Europe to resume their old tactics of sanctioning Jews, after a brief eighty-year hiatus. Indeed, Europe picked up the glove and began its own rounds of sanctions against Israeli Jews.

The mushrooming of European violence against Arabs which has reached "historic proportions" according to EU officials, was apparently not a priority for Europe anymore. That could be dealt with through rhetoric, not action. But when it comes to isolated anti-Arab violence in Israel, Europe identified an opportunity, and at some level, perhaps drew some validation and pleasure from the even slightest reversal of the principles of the American Revolution.

Repeated European Patterns

Some might think that such a depiction of European sanctions is exaggerated. After all, it is only sanctions against "a few outcast Jews, who deserve it anyway."

This was exactly the thinking during the previous assault on Judaism when European sanctions were first downplayed as "only sanctions against a few Jews, who deserve it anyway." For example, in 19th century Europe, sanctions were levied against Jews who reduced safety standards in mines they purchased, leading to the tragic death of European miners. These were viewed at first as merely against Jewish perpetrators of what was surely bad behavior, but soon the ethos of Jews dehumanizing Europeans was instilled in the broader European population. Such ethos then served as a cornerstone in the escalating incitement that led to the Holocaust.

The same happened in Spain a few hundred years earlier. At the turn of the 16th century, sanctions were imposed by the Inquisition against those Jews who had converted—taking advantage of the privilege to stay in Spain, but continuing to practice their Judaism secretly. These actions could have been downplayed as merely sanctions against a few individuals who disobeyed the arrangements—a few bad actors. But like the February 1, 2024, U.S. sanctions, this opened the doors for a broader set of sanctions against a broader set of Jews. Soon the Inquisition was targeting all "former Jews" in a concerted effort to liquidate the Jews—some by deportation and some (those who stayed in Spain and were under the jurisdiction of the Inquisition) through torture and murder.

As in previous large-scale assaults on Judaism, American Jews in the 2020s feel assured that their government is only sanctioning the "bad Jews," while they are safe in America because they are "good Jews." Some American Jews feel they even need to elevate the idea of "bad Jews" since it creates an address to direct the world assault on the Jewish nation away from them. Again, like in 20th century Germany, the view developed that the assault was not against the "good Jews" in New York, but against the "bad Jews" across the ocean. Soon, the "bad Jews" had a cohesive narrative built around them:

"EXTREMISTS ON BOTH SIDES"—INSTILLING THE COMPARISON OF HAMAS TO SETTLERS

The sanctions, U.S. and European diplomats assure us, are certainly not against Jews, and not even against Israelis. They are specifically against extremist settlers. As it is, the argument goes, settlers are violating international law and committing possible war crimes by settling on land taken in war. So even before talking about specific actions by settlers, their mere presence warrants sanctions. And yet, through the generosity of the international community, the sanctions are not (yet) directed at settlers as a whole—only at those who engage in violence.

Moreover, Palestinians are under attack by those settlers. They are the underdogs in this conflict, the narrative goes, and hence need the protection of the international community. Indeed, in 2024 the international community stepped in.

According to Biden's February 1st executive order, "The situation in the West Bank—in particular high levels of extremist settler violence, forced displacement of people and villages, and property destruction—has reached intolerable levels and constitutes a serious threat to the peace, security, and stability."

On April 18th, the EU issued a similar statement: "The European Union is gravely concerned about the worsening situation in the occupied West Bank where settler violence, intimidation, and destruction of homes and property have continued to steeply rise...."

And so, the world was led to believe that there is a widespread phenomenon called "settler violence." The facts became irrelevant. Not only are such acts of violence far less prevalent compared to "French violence" and "American violence" against Muslims, but much of the violence is perpetrated by people not living in settlements but in Israel proper, which nullifies the storyline of "settler violence." The narrative of "settler violence" runs into more trouble with realities such as "Palestinian settlers"—the thousands of Palestinians living in Jewish settlements, such as Pisgat Zeev (which Israel considers part of Jerusalem, but the U.S. and Europe consider a settlement).

Indeed, from November 2023 through mid-2024, the term "settler violence" became increasingly used in U.S. public official's speeches, including by President Biden—so much so that members of the Israeli Parliament wrote the U.S. president a letter suggesting that the term amounts to no less than a modern-day blood libel.

Indeed, the term "settler violence" is an explicit form of antisemitism, in the same way that "American Jewish sexual violence" is an explicit form of antisemitism. There is no doubt that there were American Jews who engaged in horrific sexual crimes, such as Harvey Weinstein, who was convicted of rape. There is also a widespread notion that many such crimes go unreported, especially in Hollywood. Like the Palestinian victims of violence, the American victims of sexual violence deserve protection and there is a broad consensus that such violence is intolerable. Yet, in both cases, the idea that the horrific actions of a few individuals amount to "American Jewish sexual violence" or "settler violence" is clear antisemitic hate speech and should be condemned.

The UN has quickly jumped on the "settler violence" talking point promoted by the Biden administration and pointed out that such phenomena did not start on October 7th. Indeed, in September 2023, the UN issued a report outlining acts of violence by settlers against Palestinians. (The UN never issued an extensive report about acts of violence by the French against Arabs, nor of Americans against Muslims.)

"Settler violence" became central to the global mindset. It apparently served two primary objectives. One is to underscore that, contrary to surveys showing that over 70 percent of Palestinians support the October 7th massacre, the Hamas attacks were not on behalf of the Palestinians, but merely by "extremists on both sides," just as settler violence was not committed on behalf of Israel, but by "extremists on both sides." In other words, just as there is Hamas violence against Israel, there is settler violence against Palestinians.

The second objective of instilling the perception of "settler violence" is indeed the promotion of a two-state solution, sacrosanct in Western policy circles. The two-state solution calls for the establishment of a demilitarized Palestinian state in the West Bank, where the settlements are located. While proponents of the two-state solution argue that about 80 percent of settlers would stay in their homes in "settlement blocks" in exchange for land in pre-1967 Israel, there is no doubt that the presence of settlers is a nuisance for the disciples of the two-state solution, and, as the talking-point goes, they represent "an obstacle to peace."

Therefore, vilifying the settlers is considered by some a U.S. interest, since indeed, it is not just four criminals, but the entire settlement population, that per the language of Biden's executive order, "undermine the foreign policy objectives of the United States, including the viability of a two-state solution."

Yet just as in the case of the "Office of Beggars and Jews" in 17th century France, in vilifying the settlers, the Biden administration is vilifying Israeli Jews. There is no fine line between "Israeli" and "settler," just as there is no fine line between "Upper East Side New Yorker" and "Upper West Side New Yorker." In both cases, they live in distinct areas, but the social circles are the same, the professions are the same, the places of employment are the same, the culture and identity are the same, and so are the values. They are merely New Yorkers in one case, Israeli Jews in the other.

Therefore settler violence is a refined code name for "Jewish violence." Indeed, by the spring of 2024, the US began sanctioning non-settler Jews.

The setting of the antisemitic ethos of "settler violence" gave the sanction regime against Jewish individuals legitimacy. And just as in the 1930s when sanctions progressed gradually until it became "open season on Jews," the same is true today.

CANADA FOLLOWS AMERICA'S LEAD

That "open season on Jews" was heard loud and clear by the U.S. neighbor to the north, Canada. Herzl warned against concluding that anti-Jewish rhetoric is "just words." He understood that the path to the destruction of Judaism starts with words, but then inevitably actions follow. The same happens today.

As discussed in the previous chapter, the Canadian prime minister responded to public pressure, and switched his rhetoric early on from steadfast support for the Jewish state to partaking in the ideological attack against Judaism, giving creditable certification from a head of state with access to intelligence that indeed Jews kill women, children, and babies. In doing so, Trudeau incited more of the world population against the Jews.

Yet Trudeau and his government were apparently not satisfied by supporting the *ideological* assault on Judaism. He followed by giving support for the *physical* attack on Judaism when he announced in March 2024 that he would de facto support the Hamas effort by withholding weapons from Israel. This is not word spinning. War, to a large extent, is a "zero sum game." Hamas fights with its weaponry on its side, while Israel fights with its weaponry on the other. If one wants to help one side, one can try to give them more weapons or take weapons away from the other side. Trudeau chose the latter. Canada does not supply weapons to Hamas, and the idea to begin doing so would not pass muster politically in Canada. Yet, Canada does supply weapons to Israel, and the idea of stopping is popular in Canada.

The switch to de facto aiding Hamas was an active choice that came about in two stages: On March 18, 2024, Canada's Parliament passed a nonbinding resolution to end arms exports to Israel. The motion seemed far-fetched and ludicrous, but it was worrisome that it was passed by a wide majority of 204 to 117 votes. Just as with his reaction to the masses in the restaurant, it took Trudeau one day to turn a nonbinding resolution into a binding one. On March 18, 2024, Canadian Foreign Affairs Minister Melanie Joly made the stunning announcement: Ottawa will stop future arms exports to Israel.

Canada not only helped Hamas militarily but also severely compromised the pressure on Hamas to enter a deal. It provided a morale boost and reinforced the global consciousness that the Jews were again the ones to blame. Now no longer words, now actions.

Israel, in a move somewhat similar to Margaret Thatcher's decision to close Britain's coal mines, decided a few years ago to scale down its military production capabilities and instead rely on the military production facilities of its allies, primarily in the United States. The world is flat, there is globalization, the thinking in Israel's military establishment went. Outsourcing would be more cost-efficient and our allies make superb weaponry. Who could have thought up such a crazy far-fetched scenario where our allies would use this outsourcing to prevent Israel from acquiring weapons?

Luckily, Canada is only a small component of the defense supply of Israel, with roughly USD 15 million in military exports for Israel per year. The major source of weapons is, of course, the United States, and at least in March 2024, it was broadly accepted the U.S. would never even consider an embargo on Israel, certainly not in the midst of war.

Canada, the first one to "cross the Rubicon" by switching sides on rhetoric, was also the first country "crossing the Rubicon" to stop sending weapons to Israel. But is Canada a lone actor, or will others follow? The assault on Judaism is done through sequencing; Hamas attacks, leading to the media incitement against the Jewish state, which in turn leads to government action. There was similar sequencing here: The U.S. initiated a switch from rhetoric to action by sanctioning Israeli Jews. This led Canada to switch from rhetoric to action, by effectively sanctioning the Israeli military. This in turn allows for the next step in the sequence.

By April 2024, it felt like a global ecosystem of "open season on Jews." Could this ecosystem have contributed to Iran's audacious decision to attack Israel in April with over two hundred ballistic missiles, cruise missiles, and drones?—An attack that only through what experts called a set of miracles did not cause mass casualties in Israel.

As Israelis were coming to terms with the unprecedented daring attack on the Jewish state from Iran, soon came another one—a bomb shell launched from Washington exactly a week after the Iranian attack:

U.S. SANCTIONS AGAINST THE ISRAELI ARMY

The week of April 15th was a tense one in Israel. It was compared to the so-called "anticipation days" before the 1967 Six-Day War.

As then, the enemy committed its acts of aggression (in 1967, the siege of the Straits of Tiran, in 2024, an Iranian missile and drone attack), and Israel as well as the world waited in anxious anticipation of Israel's response. As then, fears loomed that the "end of Israel," and possibly World War III would be triggered by Israel's retaliation.

On Friday morning, April 19th, the Israeli response came, reportedly the bombing of a few strategic targets in Iran. The following twenty-four hours were tense, but by Saturday night, it became clear that the exchange was over. Iran was not likely to respond further, and Israelis spent that Saturday night returning to normal.

But hours after Israelis were recovering from that episode, there was a new hit. That Saturday night, reports surfaced that the United States was planning to issue unprecedented sanctions against the Netzah Yehuda unit of the Israeli army.

Netzah Yehuda, an infantry combat unit that participated in some daring battles, is composed of Haredi Jews. Haredi (Ultra-Orthodox) Jews do not serve in the army, to a large extent because the military's secular lifestyle is perceived to be in conflict with maintaining a Haredi religious life. The Netzah Yehuda unit was designed to allow Haredim to join the army while addressing their Haredi religious requirement. Indeed, Netzah Yehuda is way more than a fine military unit composed of courageous soldiers. It is a demonstration of the unity and camaraderie of Israeli society, as well as a powerful application of the concept of inclusivity. It underscores that not only is service in the military open for everybody, but even a big organization such as the military can make accommodations to make groups with special needs feel welcome, and this in turn contributes to its own success. No doubt, Netzah Yehuda is a success story on many levels, including as a role model for those in America advocating for progressive DEI policies.

The United States' decision to sanction it came as a shock. It was soon followed by reports that three more units of the Israeli army were about to be sanctioned by the United States. Defunding a military unit in the midst of combat has both operational consequences and a demoralizing effect.

The surprises did not stop there. The following day, word came from Washington that the decision to sanction the unit had nothing to do with the Gaza War. The sanctions were for alleged behavior of individual soldiers in the unit in prior years— in particular, an incident in 2022 during an arrest operation of Palestinian suspects, when a detainee passed away, likely from a heart attack. The tragic incident was investigated by the Israeli military police and military prosecutors, leading to the discharge of two Israeli officers. Since that Palestinian detainee was an American citizen, the U.S. got involved. In addition, there were unsubstantiated reports that the sanctions were levied also because administration officials felt that some of the soldiers in the unit engaged in Islamophobic behavior or rhetoric.

Nearly every unit in any Western army has had problematic incidents during battle, and indeed nearly every unit in any Western army has had soldiers who engaged in inappropriate as well as criminal activities. For example, the U.S. Navy reported that in 2002 alone, it opened over 3,700 investigations of potential criminal activities. The Marine Corps has its own well-staffed investigation unit to investigate possible crimes committed by its soldiers. Soldiers amid battle are also aware, that as well-intentioned as they are, horrific incidents can happen, such as unintentional deaths of civilians. Soldiers are fully aware that while the vast majority of their comrades in arms act within the orders and the law, there will probably always be outcasts who do not.

Indeed, it is understood that when a Marine commits a crime, this is not the same as the Marine Corps committing a crime. Certainly, the idea that the Marines Corp or the entire Navy should face defunding due to one investigation into the criminal activity of its soldiers is absurd.

And yet, that absurdity became a reality when it came to Israel. One needs to think through this carefully: the United States government acted to defund an entire military unit, amid a war against a brutal terrorist organization—a war fought in part for the safety of the United States and its citizens. And that defunding was not undertaken because of structural problems with the unit, but because of the possibility that individual soldiers acted wrongly years earlier.

Indeed, notwithstanding its steadfast support, financial assistance, and military supply line, the Biden administration's decision to defund a unit of the Israeli army represents one of the most dramatic events in seventy-six years of the U.S.-Israeli relationship. This cannot be sugar-coated: Individuals in the Biden administration turned against brave soldiers fighting for America, not only by slandering them as the "bad guys," but by threatening to defund them, take their weapons away, give Hamas the edge, and doing so in the middle of battle.

Defunding the U.S. Military? Or Act of Antisemitism?

The decision to sanction Israeli military units could also affect the United States military. If the Biden administration is sanctioning an Israeli unit for isolated incidents years back, is it going to sanction the Marines, where cases like this are much more prevalent?

Logic should dictate that the answer is yes. While the mechanics of sanctioning Israeli military units is through the Leahy Act, which states that "no assistance shall be furnished…to any unit of the security forces of a foreign country if the Secretary of State has credible information that such unit has committed a gross violation of human rights," the administration could find another way to punish U.S. units for gross violations. After all, if one incident under investigation represents a "gross violation of human rights," then certainly 3,700 investigations must trigger the administration to do so.

Is the U.S. defunding of Netzah Yehuda a prelude to defunding the U.S. military?

The only logical way the Biden administration can avoid sanctioning American forces is if it makes clear that it is holding the Jewish state to completely different standards than other countries, including the U.S. This would fall under the Biden administration's own definition of antisemitism. Obviously, the Biden administration is holding the Jewish state to a different standard, and certainly not engaging in a "trial balloon" to defund the U.S. military.

A few days after confirming that the sanctions on the Israeli military unit are a "done deal," reports came out that the administration was backing down, at least for now. Secretary Blinken made this clear in a letter to House Speaker Mike Johnson.

This occurred two days after a fatality in a Netzah Yehuda battle with Hamas terrorists in Gaza. An Israeli soldier fighting alongside the unit as a scout was killed by Hamas. That soldier happened to be Muslim. The administration's invented narrative of an Islamophobic unit got severely damaged when a Muslim soldier fighting among its ranks—brothers next to brothers—was killed in battle.

"The Damage Is Done"

One democratic funder rationalized the reversal by saying that the sanctions were no longer needed. The mere threat of sanctions was a great accomplishment, he argued: the message was sent and now the Israeli army will "behave better" and investigate more thoroughly the violation of human rights by its soldiers.

Indeed, the mere threat of sanctions is the big event here. US sanctions demoralize Israeli Jews and suppress their self-confidence. It plays a pivotal role in the current assault on the Jewish nation. For example, this is how the event was reported in Wikipedia's entry on the Leahy Act: "In April 2024, *ProPublica* reported that Secretary of State Antony Blinken had refused to act on recommendations from the Israel Leahy Vetting Forum to sanction Israeli units that had participated in human rights violations including torture, rape, and extrajudicial killings in the West Bank."

The U.S. threat to sanction the Israeli army brought back to the public's attention the lie that Israeli soldiers are raping Palestinian women—a ludicrous allegation that was discarded even by the most radical Israel-bashers (and was even followed by an academic paper suggesting that the reason Israeli soldiers do not rape Palestinian women is due to racism). Thanks to the administration's actions, thousands of people around the world were exposed further to the slander that Israel engages in "torture, rape, and extrajudicial killings."

Indeed, the United States is now on record: Israelis are committing gross violations against human rights, exactly as Israel-bashers claimed all along. Through the mere threat of sanctions against the Israeli army, the U.S. paved the way in April 2024 for the International Criminal Court to conduct criminal investigations of Israelis and issue arrest warrants for Israeli soldiers, as well as for various other bodies to impose sanctions against Israel, moving along the path to the eradication of Judaism.

Certainly, when such actions come, President Biden will oppose them, or so the thinking was in April 2024. But even if he does, his opposition will carry a dramatically lesser weight since his administration has already determined that Israel dehumanizes Palestinians, pollutes the wells of humanity, acts as a pariah opposed by the rest of the world, and indeed, commits gross violations of human rights.

"In every generation, someone rises up to eradicate us." How arrogant was it of us to truly believe that this generation would be different, just as it was arrogant for Jews in Berlin in the 1920s to believe that their generation was different.

By May 2024, it became evident just how quickly that rise to eradicate the Jews was moving.

CHAPTER 9

"THE DAY HAS COME": THE ERADICATION BEGINS

The morning of May 19th was no different from any other morning. It was the first week after the "Days of Iyar," the early May national days, including Holocaust Remembrance Day, Remembrance Day for Fallen Soldiers and Victims of Terrorism, and Israel's Independence Day.

Just a week earlier, the president of Israel hosted the foreign ambassadors' corps at his residence in Jerusalem to mark Israel's Independence Day. As I am friends with some of those ambassadors, this was also an opportunity for me to hear their perspectives on the latest developments, as well as appreciate the personal support for Israel that they expressed privately, which at the time was very different from the official position of their governments.

Entering the reception area, the ambassadors passed by the bust of a man with a long beard—Theodor Herzl. When one of the diplomats asked me, "What's next?" I referred to the bust and shared that Herzl recognized that opposition to Judaism is chronic—it adjusts through the ages, based on evolving European and Jewish circumstances. What is next is more of this opposition, I told him.

Another ambassador reminded me of the Judaism 3.0 event we held in September 2023, just before the war and how it seemed so unimaginable back then that there was a path to the destruction of Judaism that runs through the International Criminal Court and sanctions against Israel and Israelis. Indeed, I acknowledged at that September event, after some pushback, that the path to the destruction of Judaism is not immediate—it is "someday." As it turned out, that day was not in years to come—that day arrived just one week after the president's reception.

On May 19th, the *Jerusalem Post* headline read: "The day has come: ICC seeks arrests of Netanyahu, Gallant, and Hamas chiefs."

MAY 19TH ATTACK

The International Criminal Court prosecutor stunned the world when he announced on May 19th, "Today I am filing applications for warrants of arrest before Pre-Trial Chamber I of the International Criminal Court in the Situation in the State of Palestine."

The make-believe situation he was about to outline, started with some of his first words: the State of Palestine. The international community does not recognize such a state; he personally does. It is a bit like filing arrest warrants against the president of the United States, relating to the situation in the Caliphate of Virginia. It is perhaps somewhat legitimate for the ICC prosecutor Karim Ahmad Khan to have a personal political view that Israel should not exist, and instead, have a "from the river to the sea" State of Palestine in its place, but with the power he held, even before leveling the charges, he revealed his implicit stance.

The rapes, murders, and beheadings, the ICC prosecutor insinuated, did not occur in Israel, but in the "from the river to the sea" State of Palestine. The displacement of Jews from their homes in what we (criminally?) call northern "Israel" is simply eviction of settlers from the State of Palestine. The displacement of Jews from their homes in what we (criminally?) call southern "Israel," is simply eviction of settlers from the State of Palestine.

Once the ICC prosecutor made clear his position on that, he proceeded to parrot the same accusations leveled at Jews for years: One is starvation of civilians as a method of warfare. (The "poisoning of the wells" accusation was understood as just one method the Jews used to starve Europeans.)

The other, willful killing. This was a new charge relative to the two thousand years of charges against the Jews. It was an upgrade. Until now, Jews were charged with "killing reluctantly" because they needed the blood of children to make Matzos.

But now, according to the ICC, Jewish crimes have escalated from "reluctant killing" to "willful killing."

And yet, the ICC was merely reflecting a view that by now is broadly acceptable in Western society, thanks to the media indoctrination described in previous chapters. A year prior to the war, a BBC presenter explained to her audience that the Jewish state is "happy to kill children." This was in the context of a gun battle between Islamic jihad terrorists who engaged in a number of attacks against Israeli civilians. In its battle with them, the Israeli army was able to kill the terrorists, some of them under the age of eighteen. This was enough to justify the indoctrination of the global public with the knowledge that "Israel kills children."

The BBC must have had a secret camera in Jenin that captured the smiles and joyful expressions on the Jewish soldiers' faces in the middle of a battle for their lives, being shot at by the enemy and firing back, and concluded that "Israel is happy to kill children."

The ICC accused Israeli Jews of doing just that: Willful killing. This is just one indication that Judaism today is facing a greater danger than it did a century ago. It is no longer reluctant killing—it is willful killing. It is no longer just killing children, it is being happy when killing children.

Indeed, the actions of the ICC help us understand previous episodes better. No credible historian believes that Jews actually killed children in Norwich in the 12th century to use their blood for Matzos. Similarly, no credible historian believes Jews starved Europeans by poisoning the wells of Europe in the Middle Ages—that, too, was a lie.

Yet, none of those historians were there in person. Those historians are here today. No credible historian in the future would believe the ICC's antisemitic accusation that the Jews in Israel starve Palestinian children or engage in willful killing— that is a lie. But just like back then, the lie was believed in real time—enough for the people of England to avenge the Jews by killing them, and putting public pressure on the authorities of England, who sanctioned the Jews, and eventually deported them from England!

It was the same with the case of the poisoning of the wells. That was a "fact" for millions of indoctrinated Europeans in real-time and served as a basis for an assault on Judaism then. Today as well, millions of people believe the ICC's charges of starvation and willful killing, which just adds to the long list of slanderous accusations leveled at the Jewish state by Israel-bashers.

Those lies serve as the basis for forming views about Jews and the Jewish state by people around the world. Indeed, just as in 12th-century England, and Middle-Ages Europe, the lie is the basis for the attempt to eradicate Judaism.

ISRAELI SOLDIERS' RAPE ACCUSATIONS

Lies turning into "fact" are a staple of the ideological assault on Judaism through Israel-bashing and anti-Zionism. For example, there is the accusation that Israeli soldiers and settlers engage in routine rape of Palestinian women. As discussed, this was reported in the Wikipedia entry about the April 2024 U.S. plans to sanction Israeli military units.

I recall a conversation about that with a colleague in Paris in the early 2000s. She explained to me that those things happen regularly, that I may not know about it since I am naive, and that maybe it did not occur in my military unit, but it is a widespread phenomenon that everybody knows about. Since there was no path to convince her, we "agreed to disagree." A decade later, Amnesty International "confirmed" exactly what my colleague was arguing. It accused Israel of committing sexual crimes against Palestinian women. My colleague and others were vindicated—they were right, and I was wrong. A credible source, Amnesty International, which is as credible as the ICC—validated her. The report accused Israel of sexual violence against Palestinian women. One had to read the fine print to see that Amnesty had defined sexual violence as anxiety felt when approaching a border crossing and a general sense of fear that pregnant women could have.

When it became evident that the slanderous blood-libel of Israelis raping Palestinian women was a lie invented by Israel-bashers, those who chose to believe it would not let go. They would not retract the allegation. Instead, they resorted to Plan B, which was captured in an academic paper, that was adopted by the Israel-bashing community: The reason Israeli soldiers do *not* rape Palestinian women is due to racism!

After all, if Jews are "willing killers," as the ICC certified, why would they not be "willing rapists"? Amnesty International certified that Jews commit sexual crimes. The creative explanation for this apparent contradiction?: Murder is easier—it involves pulling a trigger meters away from the target, but rape involves physical contact with the victims and the Jews who evidently are also "willing racists" do not want to have any physical contact with Palestinians.

IT'S JUST A FEW ARRESTS

It is stunning just how deep the ideological attack on Judaism has become in the 2020s, and how it translates in 2024 to plans to arrest Jews. Just as in 1920, it was stunning how deep the ideological attack on Judaism had become then, and how it translated to plans to arrest Jews, and then murder them. The ICC, as of now, is merely asking to arrest, not murder, Jews—but we are yet to know if the charges leveled against the Israeli prime minister and defense minister (as well as the infrastructure that was set in the indictment for Israeli soldiers and civilians who support them) carry the death penalty or not.

As of today, the ICC does not have the capability to impose the death penalty for crimes against humanity. But there was no death penalty in Germany in 1940 for the Jews' "crimes against humanity" either. Not yet.

Is the impact of the ICC indictments akin to the impact of the Wannsee Conference? Not as of mid-2024. But we are only at the beginning of the ICC attack, and this is just one element in the slew of mechanisms to eradicate Judaism. The others outlined in previous chapters, such as crippling sanctions, confiscation of assets, demoralization and attrition, have yet to mature as of mid-2024.

OCTOBER 7TH AND MAY 19TH UNITE ISRAELIS

Just as after the October 7th Hamas attack, Israelis came together to unite against the May 19th ICC attack. A letter was signed by nearly all members of the Israeli Parliament—the Knesset: "The IDF is the most moral army in the world. Our heroic soldiers fight with unparalleled courage and morality, in accordance with international law, as no other army has ever done.... The scandalous comparison of the prosecutor in The Hague between the leaders of Israel and the heads of the terrorist organization Hamas is an indelible historical crime and a clear manifestation of antisemitism."

It is seemingly not intuitive to unite a country in a midst of a domestic political strife, but for the Left and Right, the religious and secular, when an attempt to eradicate Judaism comes—it is indeed intuitive: We are one nation.

Israelis are united, but what about the world? Will countries around the world also label the ICC's antisemitic actions as an indelible crime? Is the world with us?

President Joe Biden assured Israelis on May 20th, the day after the ICC ideological attack, that he was with us and that he could be trusted, just as he stood with Israel on the day after the October 7th physical attack. He called the May 19th ICC action "outrageous," stating that, "There is no equivalence—none—between Israel and Hamas. We stand with Israel against threats to its security."

Is Biden standing with Israel in the way Franklin Roosevelt stood with the Jews in the 1940s? With words of sympathy but ultimately with a failure to neutralize the mechanism that led to their destruction? Roosevelt failed to act against the death camps, most notably refusing to bomb the railroad tracks that lead to them.

The ICC has been attacking Israel for years. But not just Israel—the ICC has threatened to conduct investigations against the United States, and as we can ascertain from its May 2024 actions, such investigations could involve issuing an arrest warrant for a U.S. president. Indeed, President Donald Trump responded to the ICC's previous aggression assertively: On September 2, 2020, he imposed sanctions on the ICC and on its prosecutors. In addition, the U.S. imposed restrictions on issuing visas to the U.S. for individuals "involved in the ICC's efforts to investigate U.S. personnel." That round of sanctions followed a June 11, 2020 executive order issued by President Trump that authorized the freezing of assets of ICC officials and banned ICC officials and their families from entering the United States.

Trump responded assertively to the ICC attack on the U.S., and the ICC backed down. In May 2024, as the ICC was attacking Judaism, the world awaited President Biden's reaction.

BIDEN'S ROOSEVELT MOMENT

One would assume that in the days after the ICC action, Biden was presented with a range of alternatives he could take against the ICC, including sanctions against its prosecutors, sanctions against all officials involved in bringing the attack on Judaism, and freezing assets.

But Biden could also close the ICC. Through its May 2024 action, the ICC made clear that it has become just another organization whose core business is to assault Judaism. It also has a side business of prosecuting war criminals around the world.

This is similar to the UN Human Rights Council. Its core business is assaulting the Jewish nation, but it has a side business of defending human rights around the world. In keeping with the core business, the UNHRC chose an appropriate country to chair the council's Social Forum: Iran. This makes clear what is the core and what is the side business of the UNHRC. Iran is indeed notorious for its human rights abuses, but is certainly at the forefront of the assault on the Jewish nation, and hence was apparently deemed an appropriate leader for the UN Human Rights Council.

Similarly, Hamas, Hezbollah, Al-Qaeda, and ISIS have all helped the poor, provided for the sick, and given charity to thousands of people in need. But let us not forget that their core business is terrorism.

The U.S. has the capability to shut the ICC if it so chooses. For example, it can give the Netherlands, which houses the ICC, a choice: expel the ICC from your country or lose U.S. support. (Make a choice: "ICC or DC.")

In those days in late May, as the world waited for Biden's response, a different type of response came—surprisingly or not—from Europe. As discussed, for 2,300 years, Europe has been opposing the idea of Judaism. Whatever form Judaism took, Europe was there to develop strategies and philosophies to oppose it.

Whenever Judaism was under a large-scale assault, Europe was there to support the assault. In fact, Europe played the leading role in all attempts to eradicate Judaism since the Greek attempt in the 2nd century BC. In between the round of assaults there were periods of peace, such as the "golden age" for Jews in

Europe in the last part of the 19th and early 20th century. But after each period, European opposition resumed. It is natural to think that the situation is different now. Europe and Israel are allies, and while the last round was merely eighty years ago, European governments have evolved and certainly will not lend their hand, as they did back then, to an assault on Judaism.

In the days after May 19th, Israelis were waiting: Would European countries impose sanctions on the ICC, would they join the wall-to-wall Israeli consensus, labeling the ICC actions as an antisemitic, historical crime? Or would Europe do what it has repeatedly done over the last 2,300 years: join the assault on Judaism?

EUROPEAN COLLABORATION (AGAIN)

Norway was the first to fire a shot. Its government stated: "If arrest warrant will be issued against Netanyahu and [Minister of Defense] Galant, we will be obliged to arrest them if they come to Norway." Slovenia and Ireland also expressed support.

And then came that same country that has been persecuting Jews as part of its national ethos. Like the Dreyfus affairs that defined France in the early 20th century and its collaboration with the Nazis that defined Vichy France in the mid-20th century, France made an official statement: "France supports the International Criminal Court, its independence, and the fight against impunity in all situations,"

In the 2024 choice of ICC versus Judaism, France, Norway, Ireland, and Slovenia immediately sided with ICC against the Jews. (The more it changes, the more it stays the same.) With that, the door has opened to France, Norway, and other countries to arrest the leader of the Jewish state.

This is not the first time there were arrest warrants against Jews. Indeed, when arrest warrants were issued against Jews eighty years ago, France fully complied. Many of the arrests of French Jews were not carried out by the SS or other German entities—they were carried out by French collaborators. Till this day, France, like many other European countries, hide behind the excuse that "they were just following orders." As with today's ICC, they were "obliged to arrest them".

An arrest warrant was issued—and the laws must be followed. That was France of 1940s, and sadly, that is France today.

An Act of War?

More startlingly, France is willing to partake in what some international law scholars view as an "act of war": Kidnapping another country's leader can be considered a casus belli—a cause for war. Why is it that every century Europe insists on finding some esoteric excuse to start a war?

And why is the assault on Judaism so important to France that it has taken the unthinkable step of declaring in advance, unprovoked, that it will engage in what is de facto an "act of war" against the Jewish state?

"War is the answer" has been a staple of European history since the early days of Europe. This is exactly what Herzl identified when establishing Zionism: it is not just a physical departure from Europe, it is an ideological departure from European values—one of which is the European obsession to go to war.

Herzl was so adamant about transforming Judaism away from European values, such as the chronic European addiction to war, that he even gave some trivial consideration to the idea of establishing the Jewish state in Argentina due to its considerable distance from Europe!

Herzl understood that the primary long-term problem for Zionism's advancement would be that European opposition to Judaism would follow it. He wrote: "In the first 25 years of our existence, we need, for our development, some rest from Europe, its wars and social complications."

Europe gave us barely twenty years, and then launched the region into war (see Chapter 11). And now comes French President Macron, who does not only validate the ICC's slanderous idea that Jews starve children, but also supports the ICC's response to such hideous "Jewish crimes," starting with the arrest of the Jewish state's prime minister and defense minister.

Luckily, Judaism was able to be transformed through Zionism and does not operate through the European values that Macron and France cherish. Israel will not be going to war with France. Yet Israel was reminded about the tenacity and permanence of European opposition to Judaism, as well as how far it would go to act on this opposition.

ICJ JOINS THE ASSAULT ON JUDAISM

As mentioned, the ICC is just one actor in the multinational organizations' assault on Judaism. Another prominent one is the International Court of Justice (ICJ), also based in The Hague.

On July 19, 2023, exactly two months after the ICC nulling, it issued a unique advisory opinion: "Israel's continued presence in the occupied Palestinian territory is unlawful." The court's President Nawaf Salam clarified that this includes the West Bank, Gaza, and East Jerusalem. This ruling is nonbinding, but plays a crucial role in our era's attempt to eradicate Judaism because it enables the ICC to arrest and prosecute settlers and those supporting the settlements. Moreover, legal scholars warn that it paves the path for individual countries to take their own actions, irrespective of the ICC. Imagine a Jewish family living in the Old City of Jerusalem visiting Europe. An unannounced warrant for their arrest can now be issued. Same goes for nearly a million Israeli Jews living in the areas designated by ICJ, as well as those "supporting them," which is estimate to be about nine million Israeli Jews—the entirely of the Israeli Jewish population.

Israelis visit the Western Wall, purchase products that are made in settlements, which in an integrated economy is inevitable, and employ scientists, doctors, scholars, and engineers who live in the settlements.

While the May 19th edict laid the ground for the mass arrest of Israeli soldiers, the July 19th edict laid the ground for the mass arrest of Israeli settlers.

Indeed, The Hague of 2024, the quaint Dutch town that hosts the ICC and ICJ, began to resemble more and more Wannsee of 1942, the quaint German town that hosted the conference in which the Nazis launched the "Final Solution," in last century's assault on Judaism.

CANADA FUELS THE DESTRUCTION MECHANISMS

While Israel-bashers make it no secret that supporters of war crimes are equally subject to prosecution and arrests as those perpetrating the crimes, some hoped that the legal assault would be limited to "only" soldiers, settlers, and the groups of Israeli Jews that will be targeted in future ICC and ICJ edicts, and not all Israeli Jews.

This illusion continues to be shattered as the assault on Judaism evolves. In late July, word came that Canada's Revenue Agency is about to revoke the tax-exempt statue of the Jewish National Fund—an environmental organization that is non-political and has been in the consensus of Jewish life since it was established by Theodor Herzl in 1901.

Why is the Canadian government going after the environment all of a sudden? As reported in the *Jewish Press* and in other news outlets, this was due to "the organization's support for military infrastructure in Israel."

Not only has Canada taken sides in the war on terrorism by denying Israel weapons, which inevitably supports Hamas's efforts, and prolongs the war, it is now reportedly taking the next step and sanctioning an organization simply due to the suspicion that its activities help the Israeli military efforts.

It is true that Israeli soldiers benefit from clean air, as well from the other environmental activities of the Jewish National Fund, such as the forests it plants and upkeeps. But so does the rest of the world, which the Canadian government seems to treat as "collateral damage."

I was in Quebec, the French-speaking Province of Canada, on the day that news came out. Visiting the rural countryside, I spoke to the locals, as well as to Canadians on summer vacations in the breathtaking Quebec mountain region, with its forests, rivers, and lakes. I could not help but think of the contrast between the actions of the Canadian government and the interests of its citizens I met, many of whom shared their dream to visit Israel, which they described as beautiful.

The previous day, in a speech announcing he was ending his run for reelection, President Biden underscored the importance of protecting the environment, stating that climate change "is the ultimate threat to humanity."

In effectively sanctioning the JNF, Canada defied President Biden, placing the assault on Judaism at a higher priority over preventing an "ultimate threat to humanity," as Biden called it.

Later that day, the new Democratic candidate, Kamala Harris, held a press conference talking about her meeting with Prime Minster Netanyahu. In her remarks, Harris disclosed that when she was a young girl, she collected funds to plant trees in Israel—presumably through the JNF.

People of Quebec enjoying the forests and clean air, President Biden urging humanity to protect the environment, Vice President Harris collecting money to plant trees versus Canada taking actions against the environment since it benefits the Israeli military in its war against Hamas.

Canada's JNF decision is just one example of how rapidly the assault on Judaism is expanding—one front after the other. It also underscores how other priories, such as protecting the environment, are sacrificed for the pursuit of the assault. The question in the summer of 2024 was, "what's next?"

ISRAEL ON ITS OWN (AGAIN)?

Just two weeks before the ICC action, on May 2nd, six Holocaust survivors, who were selected to light memorial torches on Israel's Holocaust Remembrance Day ceremony, met with Israeli Prime Minister Benjamin Netanyahu and his wife Sara.

One of the survivors commented that "the State of Israel is the one and only shelter for the Jewish nation." Another survivor, Michael Bar-On applied the lessons of the Holocaust by saying that "we cannot count on the world's nations that make promises."

Netanyahu responded to them: "In the Holocaust, great leaders such as Roosevelt were told what was happening in Auschwitz, Birkenau and the death camps—he was told! he knew!" Roosevelt was faced with a proposal to neutralize the death camps, such as by bombing the railroad tracks leading to them. Netanyahu recounted Roosevelt's response: "Over my dead body! I won't lose a single pilot.... Churchill, who I very much appreciate, tried to act against the death camps. His army revolted against him."

Indeed, just as Bar-On the Holocaust survivor suggested, the world's nations' inaction enabled the Holocaust. When the destruction mechanisms were activated, the Allies could have acted. They had the capabilities and the plans-of-action, but for one reason or another, decided not to act, and instead allowed the attempted eradication of Judaism to move forward....

In 2024, as the ICC destruction mechanisms were activated, Biden faced a choice: Act as President Trump did to intercept them, or act like FDR and let the assault on Judaism proceed.

In that same meeting with Holocaust survivors, Netanyahu stated that he prefers to have the world on our side, but assured them, "If we need to stand alone, we stand alone. If we do not defend ourselves, nobody will defend us."

Indeed, unlike the Holocaust and any other episode in the last two thousand years of European attempts to eradicate Judaism, the Jews have their own state, with a powerful military and a population that is geared to fight till the end. And yet, the contemporary attempt to eradicate Judaism is not done by killing Jew-by-Jew, for which a strong military can deliver an effective response. The attempt to eradicate Judaism is through the collective group elimination path—ending the idea of Judaism.

The ICC, as mentioned, is just one element in the destruction mechanisms of Judaism, but it could not have been used in isolation. As described earlier in Chapter 6, its actions came after months of incitement in the Western media shaping global public opinion against the Jews; it came after friendly governments switched their stance and joined the campaign against the

Jews; and it came after the United States "koshered" legal actions against Israeli Jews.

As the summer of 2024 progressed, the assault on Judaism deepened and expanded to more and more fronts. In France, Israeli companies were denied participation in the large Eurosatory 2024 weapons trade show, and then individual citizens of the Jewish state were denied entry, reminiscent of the "Jews Out" mantra—a common European policy for centuries. Making matters worse, a French court approved the ban on Israeli Jews, effectively giving official certification to Israel-bashing in France (the decision was later overturned in a higher court).

The summer of 2024 also saw expansion of both U.S. and European sanctions against Jews in Israel, including against individuals from the organization Tzav Tesha that includes families of hostages held by Hamas and their supporters. As roadblocking is a common practice in Israeli protests, individuals in this organization blocked the roads of aid trucks heading to Gaza, arguing they strengthen Hamas and delay the return of their loved ones. (Protests against the judicial reforms, for example, have been blocking the major highway of Tel Aviv weekly.) On August 28th, the US sanctioned the Chief Security Officer of Yitzhar, a settlement that has been the target of numerous terrorist attacks, as well as a volunteer organization that was accused of providing support to those sanctioned in previous rounds.

A joke emerged in Mahane Yehuda Market, Jerusalem's vibrant social scene where people of all ages and backgrounds shop, eat, and drink. When it is time to pay the bill with a credit card, the merchant says: "Now let's see if you too were sanctioned by Biden."

Also in August, the UK, which brought a legal challenge against the ICC's outrageous actions, retracted its objection. The

United Kingdom understood that the ICC action creates a dangerous precedent that can be used against the UK as well. Many in British politics and civil service watched the film *The Ghost Writer*, where the prime minister of the United Kingdom is charged with war crimes. The ICC indictment against the Israeli prime minister makes the fiction plot one step closer to reality, and exposes UK's own soldiers to ICC prosecution. Yet, following the July 4th victory of the Labor Party and formation of a new government, the UK retracted this challenge. Evidently, protecting British soldiers, its political leaders, its allies, and its own moral principles is not the priority. Allowing the ICC to move forward in its assault on Judaism evidently is. By August, reports came out that the United Kingdom was considering following Canada and blocking arm shipments to the Jewish state.

This came as a surprise, since the Labor Party was said to have "cleaned up" since its antisemitic pro-Hamas days of Jeremy Corbyn during the 2010s.

If it is true that the UK is giving backwind to the 21st assault on Judaism, it would be "déjà vu" of what happened in the 20th century assault on Judaism.

Then too, the UK was at first adamantly pro-Jewish, having received a mandate from the League of Nations to usher in a Jewish homeland in Palestine. For that, Israelis are forever grateful, and indeed have streets named for British Prime Minster David Lloyd George's and his foreign minister Arthur Balfour. In fact, the official residence of the Israeli prime minister is on Balfour Street in Jerusalem.

But then, as the genocide of Jews in Europe began, the United Kingdom reneged on its obligation under international law, and blocked Jewish immigrations to Palestine. These British actions forced Jews to be in Europe, and doomed them to their death.

Speaking with Lloyd George's great-granddaughter, the renowned World War I historian Margaret MacMillan, she explained to me that Britain was acting out of its own narrow interest: "They were operating under a mandate, but did not think this would really lead to full independence so quickly. They thought it would just stay part of their empire," she shared in a 2017 *Jerusalem Post* interview. Indeed, like France, the United Kingdom too has yet to come to terms with its role in the 20th century assault on Judaism, and it seems, as of August 2024, that it is getting ready to partake in the 21st century assault on Judaism.

As the summer of 2024 was ending, it seems that Bar-On the Holocaust survivor was right: Israel cannot count on the world's nations and is increasingly on its own.

In the last week of August, the EU's Borrell escalated further, announcing a new initiative that will essentially "cancel" the Israel electorate: Imposing sanctions against a number of elected government ministers of the Jewish state who Borrell does not like the way they speak (what he referred to as "hate speech", per his own judgment). In the following days, he began a campaign to draft European governments to partake in his Jewish suppression initiative.

It became evident that the pace of the 2024 assault on Judaism is significantly faster than that of the assault in the 20th century.

By September 2024, it was clear: Indeed, there is an imminent threat to Judaism.

"In every generation, someone rises up to eradicate us" is right now.

SAVING JUDAISM

CHAPTER 10

DISRUPTING THE PATH TO DESTRUCTION

The common theme of all Jewish holidays, "They tried to kill us," is followed by, "We survived, let's eat." In the previous chapters, we discussed the "they tried to kill us" of our era. In the following chapters, we will outline the template to get us to "we survived."

A prerequisite to putting together an effective defense strategy against a large-scale assault involves three basic elements: acknowledging that indeed there is an assault, determining who is committing the assault, and identifying what is the arena in which the assault is being carried out.

In the October 7th physical assault on Judaism, it was quite clear: We were indeed under a large-scale assault, it is being carried out by Hamas, and the arena was Gaza.

The same clarity exists for the ideological assault on Judaism: We are indeed in the midst of a large-scale assault on Judaism and it is coming from the West. In the last few years, my discussions of such threats were in the realm of "hypothetical." In the aftermath of October 7th, it became clear: the assault on Judaism is live and the arena for the attack on Judaism is Zionism and the Jewish state.

THE POINT OF ATTACK ON JUDAISM: ZIONISM

As discussed, Zionism is not the reason for the attack on Judaism. It is the vehicle through which the assault on Judaism is being made. That is because Zionism has become the anchor of Judaism.

Historically, large-scale attacks on Judaism have always been carried out through the most relevant aspect of Judaism of that time. When Judaism was anchored in the Temple, the Greeks tried to eradicate Judaism by desecrating the Temple, and the Romans by burning it. When Jews were organized in insular communities and bound together through the religious aspect of Judaism, the assault on Judaism was carried out through its theological and religious aspects. When Jews were given rights and lived freely in Europe, the attack was on the emancipated Jews—their success, freedom, and power.

The wrong defense strategy against the 20th century assault on Judaism would have been defending Judaism's religious merits, which was no longer the arena in which the attempt to eradicate Judaism was being conducted. There was no point trying to convince a Nazi officer coming to arrest a Jew that Jews did not kill Jesus. The Nazis did not care. True, previous attempts to destroy Judaism were based on such religion-related accusations, but not in the 20th century.

The Nazis' assault on Judaism was based on a new ideology of the time, which by the end of the 19th century was given a new name: antisemitism. After October 7th, it is clear that the contemporary assault on Judaism is based on the relatively new ideology of Israel-bashing.

Sadly, in the decades leading to the Holocaust, many Jews failed to recognize that the attack was no longer based on religious opposition to Judaism as it was in previous centuries; today, many fail to realize that the attack is no longer based on traditional antisemitism, as it was in the 20th century. Israel-bashing and anti-Zionism have replaced traditional antisemitism as the vehicle of opposition to Judaism, as more and more of the world's touch-points with Judaism are now through Israel and Zionism.

Theodor Herzl, the father of Zionism, wrote: "How can we tell the power of an idea? When we see that nobody can ignore it—whether he is for it, or against it."

Zionism today is the one aspect of Judaism that cannot be ignored, including, as Herzl acknowledged, in opposition. Indeed, criticism of Israel has become the number one Jewish-related activity for many American Jews, by far—more than going to synagogue, thinking about the Holocaust, or engaging in Jewish cultural activities. Social media posts like "As a Jew, I am embarrassed about Israel" are indicative that it is Zionism, just as Herzl envisioned, that brings Jews back into their Judaism.

It is quite simple: Zionism has become the anchor of Judaism, and that is why the assault on Judaism is carried out though Zionism and the Jewish state.

The Attack Cannot Be Fended Off Through Public Relations

Herzl mocked "Committees against antisemitism." They were futile, he argued, since dogmatic minds cannot be changed. The same can be said today about Israeli public diplomacy, known in Hebrew as "Hasbara."

Israel can put its most eloquent speakers on CNN, and the BBC; influencers can take the cause to Twitter, Instagram, and Facebook; Israel's advocates can hold debates, symposiums, and press conferences—but this will not alter the magnitude of the core threat. After all, who are you going to believe—a credible BBC journalist or a Zionist settler?

In that July 2023 interview when the BBC presenter stated to her audience that Israel was "happy to kill children," the person on the other side of the screen was former Israeli prime minster Naftali Bennett, one of Israel's most eloquent spokespersons. He should have had an "easy win": Israel was in the midst of a brutal battle in Jenin against Islamic Jihad terrorists who had been engaging in murder, roadside shooting, and fighting against "moderate" Palestinians. Israeli forces operating in Jenin successfully eliminated quite a few terrorists. Some of them, as it was reported, were not yet eighteen years old. This was the basis of "happy to kill children" slander. Not bombing in Gaza, not "starvation," not "extrajudicial killing," but defending against murderers who were under the age of eighteen.

Still, if one had to take a survey of public sentiment following that interview, it is likely that viewers still believed that Israel killed Palestinian children. This is because whether we like it or not, the respectable BBC presenter was indeed more credible to the world than a former prime minister, a Zionist, who was also the former head of the National Religious Party, and once held the position of director general of the Judea and Samaria Council, the organization which represents the Jewish settlements in the West Bank. (To use the jargon from the BBC memo, it was credible BBC reporter vs "Settler Colonialist.")

In crafting a defense of Judaism, just as it is important to acknowledge that there is a large-scale assault and that the aspect of Judaism being attacked is Zionism, it is also important to admit that the attack cannot be fended off through "committees against Israel-bashing." In crafting such a defense, one needs not only to be strategic and aim for long-term impact but also to have the discipline to abandon old templates and conceptions that are no longer relevant in the current assault on Judaism.

STOPS ALONG THE PATH TO DESTRUCTION

In previous chapters, we outlined the path to the destruction of Judaism and showed how we are already far along this path. To save Judaism, we need to intercept that path-of-destruction. That can be done by focusing on the various stops along this path:

-The hard-core Israel-bashers who are leading the assault on Judaism through "pro-Palestinian" activities and the slander of the Jewish state and its citizens.

-The Israel-basher-lites, who may not be organic Israel-bashers, but are influenced by incitement in the media and by the pressure of the hard-core Israeli-bashers

-Governments that ultimately have the capability to activate the destruction mechanisms of Judaism, but also have the capabilities to defend Judaism.

Each group along this path has its unique motivations, characteristics, and vulnerabilities, and for each, a different strategy must be tailored.

<u>Hard-Core Israel-Bashers</u>

The hard-core Israel-bashers are the ones who drive public opinion against the Jews. They are the face of the assault on Judaism. They carry the "From the river to the sea" banners, they accuse Israel of genocide, of committing a holocaust. They take over college campuses and disrupt lectures of Israeli speakers. They are the most vocal part of the assault on Judaism.

Yet, they do not possess the destruction mechanism.

While they are not a homogenous group, the crux of that part of the assault on Judaism is mostly young progressives, driven by DEI (diversity, equality, inclusion) and woke values. They are characterized by strong conviction, making it hard to "convince" them of anything. To their credit, most of them act based on a strong belief that they are doing the right thing, per their understanding of the world.

While they have strong convictions, most of them lack substance. They are not acting based on firsthand experience or independent research, but rather on secondhand soundbites they get from their social networks, their friends, and their "clergy" (be they progressive professors, liberal news organizations, popular social media influencers, or opinion leaders). They express their opposition to Judaism through being "pro-Palestinian," which in their social circles is akin to being pro-women, pro-minorities, or pro-justice.

A Catalan separatist once told me that the primary problem of their separatist movement is that they are occupied by Spain and not by Israel. If they were occupied by Israel, the entire world would be pro-Catalonia, and nobody would have ever heard of Palestine.

Indeed, most of those hard-core Israel-bashers waving a Palestinian flag could not find Palestine on a map. It has become a culture, a fashion, and a trend. This, for example, was expressed in the September 2023 University of Pennsylvania festival, "Palestine Writes." For an American to write about a longing for a physical Palestine that he has never been to, nor heard much about, is rather absurd. However, he can write about injustice, about how he can imagine life under occupation, about the travesty of oppression, the cancer of fascism, and the malaise of Zionism—and by extension of Judaism—which, after all, represents a counter-diversity, counter-inclusivity concept to him.

For them, the assault on Judaism through the Western pro-Palestinian movement is driven by their opposition to colonialism, racism, the suppression of basic human freedoms, and the violation of human rights.

The way to address this group is to demonstrate, that the Western pro-Palestinian movement is a colonialist movement that hijacked the plight of Palestinians for its own benefit.

While the intention of many western pro-Palestinians is good, they should be aware that when they wave their Palestine flag, put on their keffiyeh, and head to the protest, they are engaging in Islamophobia, bigotry, and white colonialism. (See Chapter 11.)

Israel-Basher-Lites

The Israel-basher-lites are not by their nature antisemitic. They may have no organic interest in the assault on Judaism. But they are influenced by the pressures created by the hard-core Israel-bashers and act on it.

Unlike the hard-core Israel-bashers who show their opposition mostly through rhetoric since they do not have a destruction mechanism, the Israel-basher-lites can assault Judaism in both rhetoric and actions. This is because Israel-basher-lites are the ones who possess the destruction mechanisms of Judaism. They are normative people in government, media, international organizations, and places that can inflict damage on Judaism. Some of them are my friends.

They are driven by public sentiment and their assessment of where "the wind is blowing." Many in this group serve the public and therefore seek to accommodate public opinion. The politicians in this group need to get reelected; civil servants need to execute the will of those they serve; journalists need to provide information to the public—and as that journalist who rationalized the distorted headline "Israel kills dozens of Palestinians" put it, "this is what Europeans want to hear."

This group is not only normative, but they want to stay normative. They are therefore sensitive to social pressures. They do not wish to separate from the prevailing wisdoms and the presumed principles of their milieu. As a result, this group is easily influenced by incitement against the Jewish state—whether it comes from the media, college campuses, or their social circles.

They may not have initiated any anti-Jewish action themselves, such as imposing sanctions on Israeli Jews or slandering Israel, but they would in reaction to, or as an outcome of, political considerations. Would those in the U.S. government who pushed the idea to sanction Israeli Jews have done so had there been no incitement? Would Secretary Blinken have implied that the Jews in Israel dehumanize others had the public not been crying that for months? Would Justin Trudeau have accused Jews in Israel of killing women, children, and babies had he not been assaulted the previous day at a restaurant, seen all the Palestinian flags waving in Canadian cities, followed the anti-Israel coverage in the media, and experienced intense anti-Jewish pressure in his social circles? Highly doubtful.

Israel-basher-lites are not "organic Israel-bashers"; they are "reactionary Israel-bashers."

Mostly, they operate under the assumption that their participation in the assault on Judaism is not antisemitic. Unlike the hard-core Israel-basher, the one thing the normative Israel-basher-lite fears is being perceived as an antisemite. While being anti-Zionist and an Israel-basher is socially acceptable and even encouraged in certain circles, being anti-Jewish is a career-ending taboo. Therefore, once there is a broad recognition that Judaism has transformed and Zionism is now its anchor, Israel-bashing becomes Jew-bashing. This deters the attacks and alters the nature of the existential threat to Judaism. (See Chapter 12.)

The following table summarizes the bifurcated strategies to deal with those two groups, each on their own level on the path-of-destruction, as will be discussed in Chapters 11 and 12:

	Hard-Core Israel-Basher	Israel-basher-lite
Threat	• Sets public opinion	• Activates destruction mechanisms
Motive	• DEI, Woke	• Public Sentiment
Assumption	• Their Israel-bashing actions are expressions of DEI/Woke	• We are in Judaism 2.0
Characteristics	• Fringe • High conviction, low substance • Not driven by pro-Palestinian but by anti-Israel • Immune to accusations that they are antisemites	• Normative • Low conviction, high substance • Risk-averse • Sensitive to accusations of being antisemites
Fear	• Being perceived as colonialists, counter-woke, and counter-DEI • Being rejected as an outcast by their peers	• Being perceived as an antisemite • Lose job/position/public image; be scolded by the media
Countering	• Understand that their actions are colonialist, Islamophobic, and racist	• Understand that the world is in Judaism 3.0

<u>Governments</u>

The final stop in the path to destruction of Judaism lies with governments. Israel-bashers can issue arrest warrants against Israelis, but they are only effective if governments enforce them. Indeed, all previous large-scale assaults came through the actions of governments.

Haman set up a path to eradicate Judaism, but his plans went into action only because the Persian government decided to go along. Had King Achashverosh said no, the plan would not have moved forward. The English public was outraged at the Jews for their alleged practice of killing their children and using their blood to make Passover Matzos. This could have led to prolonged violence, murder, and rape against the Jews. However, the plan to fully and completely eradicate any traces of Jewish life in England could have only moved forward if the English government had decided to do so.

Certainly, the last attempt to eradicate Judaism would not have moved forward had it not been for the German government. They are the ones who controlled the German military and directed the resources for the "final solution"—their plan to eradicate Judaism by killing Jew-by-Jew. The same is true today. The success of the assault on Judaism depends on governments.

Yet unlike previous attempts to eradicate Judaism, there is one unique powerful country in the Western world founded in Judeo-Christian principles. And unlike in the mid-20th century attempt to eliminate Judaism, that country—the United States of America—has enormous leverage over nearly all European and Western governments, should it decide to use it.

Moreover, the assault on Judaism is also an assault on Americanism. As discussed in Chapter 13, the assault on Judaism is an assault on the Judeo-Christian values in which America is rooted and is an attempt to negate the principles of the American revolution. Moreover, the assault on Judaism destabilizes the world and is a national security threat to the United States. The infrastructure that is set to arrest Israeli soldiers and political leaders can also serve as a "plug and play" template to be used against American soldiers and political leaders.

In the last go-round, the United States had the capabilities to neutralize or at least sabotage the destruction mechanisms of Judaism. President Roosevelt chose not to do so. Today the United States has the capabilities to neutralize or at least sabotage the destruction mechanisms of Judaism, such as through sanctioning the ICC and its collaborators.

CHAPTER 11

ARENA SHIFTING: BRING THE BATTLE TO THE ISRAEL-BASHERS' TURF

The most effective way to defend against the attack from hard-core Israel-bashers is to bring the battle to them.

This is exactly what Theodor Herzl did when he was ready to defend Judaism from the new existential threat that was percolating in his time—antisemitism. When he met the German Kaiser, Wilhelm II, he did not try to dissuade him of his antisemitic views. Instead, he brought the battle to him, using the Kaiser's own language and beliefs.

The Kaiser was concerned about growing "Jewish influences" in German society and culture. Instead of arguing that this was an exaggerated antisemitic view, Herzl provided the Kaiser with the solution to his concerns using the Kaiser's own framework: The Jews would exert their influence in the Jewish state instead of in the German state. Moreover, the Jews would dwell in German culture there as opposed to in Germany, since the Jewish state would be a German protectorate.

The Kaiser was concerned about the threat of Socialism, and he viewed Jews as a driving force in the Socialist movement that was a threat to his rule. Once again, Herzl did not try to demonstrate to the Kaiser that the Jews were loyal subjects and that only a minority of them were Socialists. Instead, he showed how their Socialist ideas could be put to better use in the Jewish state, and later, if successful, be implemented in other countries, should those countries choose to do so. For example, the seven-hour work day was a Socialism-friendly template Herzl had developed and envisioned for the Jewish state—it would both increase output and please the Socialists.

The Kaiser and his government were also concerned about Jews in Germany fueling domestic tensions, since Jews—now emancipated, educated, and successful—were taking away Germans' jobs and lucrative positions, purchasing real estate, and competing against German-owned businesses. Herzl did not try to refute those antisemitic allegations. Instead, he provided a solution catering to the Kaiser's interests: If a substantial number of Jews moved out of Germany, there would be less competition, and domestic tensions would naturally be reduced. If Jews used their capital to buy real estate in the Jewish state instead of in Germany, there would be less pressure on the German real estate market.

Herzl believed that the Kaiser was failing to acknowledge the enormous degree of contribution that Jews were making to Germany. As loyal subjects of the Kaiser, Jews were productive members of society. But Herzl had the self-discipline to understand there was no point in arguing with the Kaiser. He understood that being defensive and refuting allegation by allegation, would not be effective after centuries of antisemitic indoctrination. Instead, he brought the battle to the Kaiser, on the Kaiser's turf, antisemitism. Herzl used the antisemites' own logic to accomplish what he set out to do: Get the Kaiser's endorsement and advocacy for a Jewish state.

Some three years earlier, Herzl had a beer in Paris with famed Jewish philosopher Max Nordau. They both agreed that European persecution of Jews was chronic and had defined Judaism; they both agreed that the solution would be the reestablishment of the Jewish state, but they had a disagreement: Nordau thought antisemitism would be an insurmountable hurdle in the quest for a Jewish state. Herzl understood that he could turn antisemitism into an asset.

A similar strategy should be deployed today in countering the hard-core Israel-bashing movement—those on college campuses, in European public squares, and on social media who are taking pride in being part of the western pro-Palestinian movement, viewing it as an outgrowth of progressive woke and DEI ideals, carrying Palestinian flags and "End the Genocide" banners.

21ST CENTURY COLONIALISM

Let's say it outright: The Western pro-Palestinian movement is one of the greatest manifestations of white colonialism in our time.

Western "pro-Palestinians" exploit the suffering of Palestinians to promote their own agenda. There is a structural disconnect between the interests of the Palestinians and that of their Western "supporters"—many of whom cannot point to Palestine on a map.

Palestinians and pro-Palestinians are two different, competing movements. They have different long-term objectives, short-term goals, cultures, symbols, ethos, mottos, and banners. In the clash between the interests of pro-Palestinians and Palestinians, it is clear who wins. The Western pro-Palestinian movement is well-funded, organized, and structured, with access to resources and power.

For example, take the basic human right to choose where to work. An individual who receives a job offer, should be able to accept or reject it. He might have complex considerations to take into account, but at the end of the day, it is his decision.

Palestinians believe that they should have that right, like any other human. But Western pro-Palestinians do not believe that Palestinians should have that right.

Denying Palestinians the Freedom of Employment

The Western pro-Palestinian movement estimates that the unemployment rate in the Palestinian territories is over 50 percent. But at the same time, they are at the forefront of sabotaging Palestinian employment in Jewish-owned businesses. For example, Jewish-owned SodaStream had a factory in the West Bank that employed both Israelis and Palestinians. Some Palestinians held management positions, and some had been working in the company for years.

The pro-Palestinian movement and its partner, the European Union, placed intense pressure on SodaStream to shut its factory in the West Bank and move it inside the Green Line. SodaStream is an international company, with sales all over the world, including in Europe. Given the pressure from European governments and the EU, SodaStream caved and closed its West Bank factory.

This was a great victory for the Western pro-Palestinian movement. It is used as an example of how protests, taking to the streets with banners, and wearing a keffiyeh can have an impact. The public pressure led European governments and the EU to take this strong stance against Israeli "colonialism" and close that West Bank factory. They are right: The campaign was successful and the Jewish-owned company closed its factory—and as a result, five hundred Palestinians lost their jobs.

This is just one instance of how helpless Palestinians are, relative to their powerful pro-Palestinian adversaries (who pretend to be their supporters).

It is an example of the European mantra of "Palestinians last, conflict first." Palestinians lost their jobs, leading to an even higher rate of Palestinian unemployment. The Israel-bashers ("pro-Palestinians") benefit from this suffering of the Palestinian Arabs and exploit it. With this rise in unemployment, and the increased economic hardship the fired employees face, the pro-Palestinian movement gains more opportunity to show the West how brutal the occupation is, as well as to incite Palestinians against Israel.

One day you are a manager in a SodaStream factory, the next day you are sitting at home wondering how to feed your children—the realities of Jewish colonialism! Beyond the economic damage, the Israel-bashers disenfranchise the Palestinians, denying them their personal self-determination, and robbing them of their ability to make their own employment decisions. It is arguably legitimate for the West to try to convince a Palestinian not to work in a Jewish-owned company in the settlements, but who has the ultimate choice?

Human-rights principles would say: the Palestinian. The Western Pro-Palestinian would say: The Western pro-Palestinians.

When confronted with this dichotomy, Westerners, including those engaging in the campaign to block Palestinians from working in Jewish-owned companies, rationalize it in two ways:

One involves pulling out some Western legalese: According to section so-and-so in the convention on human rights of so-and-so, denial of employment is defined as this and that… it is hard to follow, but just as Amnesty International found a section in some code that can be twisted to prove that a pregnant woman's anxiety should be defined a sexual crime perpetrated by Israel, the same can be done here. Do the Palestinians who lost their jobs care about section so-and-so in the convention of so-and-so? Did they even hear about it?

This leads to the second argument frequently offered by members of the Conflict-Industry who work closely with Western "pro-Palestinians": Palestinians are under occupation. The Israeli occupation corrupts their judgment. They do not have the ability to decide whether to work for the Jewish-owned company or not. We, white Europeans, on the other hand, see the big picture and from the luxury of the pubs of London or cafes of Paris, can decide this for the Palestinians.

The mechanism: Apply pressure by deploying European tax-payers' euros to force SodaStream to close their factory in the West Bank. This of course is for the benefit of those misguided Palestinians. In other words, we pro-Palestinians are here to "overrule" mistakes the Palestinians make, such as the misinformed decision to work at the SodaStream factory.

Such colonialist thinking of the pro-Palestinian movement is a byproduct of their obsessive assault on Judaism. Indeed, Palestinians are the victims of Israel-bashers. One needs to wonder: That western Pro-Palestinian demonstrating in London, wearing a keffiyeh and holding a banner, "Stop the Genocide in Palestine"—does he ever think of his Palestinian victims? Does he ever wonder what his assault on Judaism is doing to the Palestinian who lost his job, income, and human rights "thanks" to him?

But pro-Palestinian colonialists do not stop at employment. They follow their Palestinian victims to the store. If Palestinians are so misguided (due to the occupation) that they wish to be employed and mentored in a Jewish-owned company, then they might be deluded into purchasing products from Jewish-owned stores. Therefore, it is not just employment, but also consumption that must be suppressed by western pro-Palestinians—of course for the Palestinians' own good.

Denying Palestinians the Freedom of Consumption

The UN Human Rights Council, like the ICC, is an organization whose core business is the assault on the Jewish nation. Just as the ICC has a side business of prosecuting world criminals around the world, the UN Human Rights Council has a side business of protecting human rights around the world.

The core business consumes much of their resources, energy, and budget. Their side business is mostly an afterthought. When Nikki Haley was the U.S. ambassador to the UN, she referred to the UN Human Rights Council, as a "protector of human rights abusers." After all, its member states are countries like Cuba and Rwanda. In 2023, the UNHRC took a step further in underscoring what its core business is by appointing Iran to be the chair of its 2023 Social Forum.

Does that mean the United Nations considers hanging gays from cranes to be an expression of human rights? Of course not. But the UNHRC is not about human rights, it is about assaulting Judaism, and Iran is a suitable leader for this role.

In 2021 the UNHRC faced a decision that had competing and opposite consequences for its two lines of business: It would have helped its core business of assaulting Judaism but would have hurt its side business of protecting human rights—in this case, the human rights of Palestinians. The UNHRC made the obvious choice—pursue the objective of assaulting Judaism, and sacrifice the human rights of Palestinians. Indeed, the UNHRC effectively decided to suppress the Palestinian freedom of consumption.

The assault on Judaism here was done by bullying companies around the world to violate their own morality and business interest and stop them from selling merchandise to Jewish residents of the West Bank. The UNHRC therefore began composing a blacklist of hundreds of international companies that currently do so. The UNHRC then took the bullying a step further by initiating a "dialogue" with those companies to persuade them to change course.

The consequence of ending sales in the West Bank does not have a significant impact on Israelis, but it certainly does on Palestinians. Unlike Israeli residents of the West Bank, Palestinians do not have access to shopping centers within the Green Line. Many of them depend on shopping in settlements, such as the Rami Levy supermarket in Gush Etzion. The attempt to disenfranchise the Palestinians from their human right to shop as they please is not just the action of a few "pro-Palestine" activists who put their own interests ahead of the Palestinians— it is an organized campaign, led by the Office of the UN High Commissioner for Human Rights.

Whether in Brussels or Geneva, Western "pro-Palestinians" thousands of kilometers away are making decisions for Palestinians—the ultimate expression of Western colonialism.

<u>Suppression of Palestinians' Property Rights</u>

The colonialist efforts of pro-Palestinians to disenfranchise Palestinians is also reflected in their attempt to negate their right to choose where to live.

Some Palestinians provoke the EU and pro-Palestinian colonialists, by choosing to live in Jewish settlements. For example, the Palestinian population in the north Jerusalem neighborhoods of Pisgat Ze'ev and French Hill, considered by the international community as settlements since they are beyond the pre-1967 lines, is estimated to be as high as 10 percent of the total population! (Some are Israeli-Arabs studying or working in Jerusalem, but many are Palestinians who moved from the Arab to the Jewish neighborhoods of Jerusalem.)

"Pro-Palestinian" colonialists are eager to stop such "sacrilegious" behavior. European diplomats have been leading the charge to block the construction of Givat Hamatos, a joint Israeli-Palestinian neighborhood located beyond the pre-1967 lines and hence qualifying for the golden European designation of "occupation." As in previous episodes of European colonialism, the Europeans prioritize their own values over the Palestinians' human right to choose. Palestinians in nearby Beit Safafa wish to purchase homes in this new modern neighborhood.

EU officials explain that the new neighborhood "would cut off east Jerusalem from Bethlehem and severely undermine future negotiations toward a two-state solution in line with the internationally agreed parameters." Not only does the EU ignore long-standing realities on the ground, such as the established Jerusalem neighborhoods of Gilo and Har Homa that border Bethlehem and already "cut off East Jerusalem from Bethlehem," but it also prioritizes what it calls "international parameters" over the human rights of local Palestinians to choose.

This is a staple of pro-Palestinians' colonialist behavior: Their concern is Western frameworks, principles, and slogans, not the Palestinians.

Suppression of Palestinians' Right to Control Their Assets

Pro-Palestinian colonialists' disenfranchisement of Palestinians' right to make residential choices also happens in reverse. A Palestinian selling his home to a Jew is considered taboo in Palestinian circles. Yet, for the western pro-Palestinian, this amounts to "self-imposed ethnic cleansing."

While the 2024 Hamas war slogan provided by Western media is "Ceasefire Now," in 2011, it was "ethnic cleansing." Hamas claimed that Jewish ownership of property in the predominately Arab neighborhoods of Jerusalem was a legitimate excuse to fire over 4,300 rockets at Israeli cities in May 2021. While the EU, like most of the West, condemned Hamas terrorism, it still provides legitimacy to the Hamas rhetoric, resorting to the usual "we condemn, but."

On the one hand, we have Hamas firing rockets, but on the other hand, per the EU in 2021, we have "the increase in evictions and demolitions across the occupied Palestinian territory, notably the evolving situation in Sheikh Jarrah and Silwan, in east Jerusalem, and the possible demolition of structures in the Palestinian village of Walaja, are also alarming."

A Sami in Lapland is allowed to sell his property to Norwegian "settlers." (Is the EU planning to invest billions of euros to address the "ethnic cleansing" of the Sami in Scandinavia?) The same holds for Catalans selling property to Spaniards in Barcelona, and German "natives" to Muslims in Cologne. But per the colonialist stance of the EU and pro-Palestinian movement, Palestinians' property rights—like their employment rights and purchasing rights—are apparently subject to a racial test.

Humanity advances, populations and neighborhoods evolve, but when it comes to Palestinians, Europe seems to be stuck in the mindsets of previous centuries. To state it simply: For the EU and the pro-Palestinian activists, property laws do not apply to Palestinians. They do not apply when a Palestinian wishes to defy Europe and buy an apartment in a Jewish neighborhood. It does not apply when a Palestinian wishes to defy Europe and sell his property to a Jew—per the EU, that is self-imposed ethnic-cleansing.

By the same token, the Western European Colonialist stance is that property laws do not apply to Palestinians who choose to build a house on their neighbor's orange grove, in a public park, or by the side of the road. If a European Muslim (or non-Muslim) built a house in the middle of London's Hyde Park or the parking lot of Paris' Eiffel Tower, he would be evicted and that structure would be demolished. However, the EU has been encouraging Palestinian Muslims to do just that. And in recent years, the amount of unlicensed unauthorized Palestinian construction has mushroomed, to the tune of millions of European taxpayers's euros. If those makeshift homes collapse, it will of course be Israel's fault for not enforcing safety standards as the "occupying power" per some section of some convention.

The name of the game forced by the European Union and Western pro-Palestinians activists on Palestinians is "land-grab." Indeed, in particular, there have been attempts to build as close as possible to Jewish settlements to prevent them from expanding. Reportedly, Europeans pay Palestinians to build a house, an agricultural structure, or even plant a tree, and then wait to see if Israel issues a warrant to demolish it. If it does, the lengthy court proceeding gets covered by the Western media and such demolition is then deemed by the EU as "ethnic cleaning."

A lot has been said about "Pallywood"—about how the Palestinian cause is orchestrated in Western media (such as in coordinated "spontaneous" riots.) But there is much to say about "EuroWood"—the European orchestration of big parts of the Israeli-Palestinian conflict, and that includes financially incentivizing Palestinians to build a hut or plant a tree "that belonged to your grandfather" by Jewish residential areas, by roads, and wherever instructed by the European patrons.

Hamas's terrorist action in reaction to such eviction can then be condemned, but qualified that it was "not in a vacuum" (the good old "we condemn, but"), the ICC can have new material for its war crimes script, and pro-Palestinians in London, Paris, and U.S. college campuses get housing demolitions, and another reason to protest.

Pro-Palestinian colonialism is not limited to employment, consumption, and residence. It extends into terminology, such as the term "ethnic cleansing." For Palestinians "ethnic cleansing" is about the 1948 displacement from villages like Sheikh Muwannis and Al-Haram, now respectively Ramat Aviv, home to Tel Aviv University, and Herzliya, home to the villas of Western diplomats. For Western pro-Palestinians, this is about the 2021 eviction of seven Palestinian families in a property dispute or the 2024 displacement of Palestinians in Gaza.

UN employees often do not refer to Palestine by name—that would be too easy on Israel because it would miss one of the key aspects of the Western narrative of what is Palestine. Instead, the UN as well as many NGOs in the Conflict-Industry refer to it as OPT—Occupied Palestinian Territories. Have any Palestinians ever heard of OPT?

Indeed, just like Western pro-Palestinians cannot point to Palestine on the map, Palestinians cannot point to OPT on the map.

PRO-PALESTINIAN RACISM

As discussed, the language, ethos, symbols, and banners of pro-Palestinians are different than those of Palestinians, starting with the flagship banner of the pro-Palestinian movement: the Keffiyeh.

The Keffiyeh is today's blackface. It is a stereotype of an Arab from the previous century—not of today. It is not too different than using one's finger to stretch one's eyes to emulate an Asian or painting one's face with black shoe polish.

Let's be clear, there was a time when blackfacing was tolerated and even popular. Moreover, it was used to show support to African Americans. In 1993, *Cheers* star Ted Danson wanted to support his then-girlfriend Whoopi Goldberg at an event held in her honor, so he showed up with his face painted black. At the time this drew sharp criticism—and was deemed racism. By 2019, when news broke that Virginia Governor Ralph Northam had appeared in a photo in his 1984 yearbook with his face painted black he was asked to resign. (He apologized and kept his position.)

Indeed, those wearing a keffiyeh are not showing support for Palestinians, they are engaging in bigotry and Islamophobia. The keffiyeh today does play a role, and that is to cover one's face when engaging in terrorism. The keffiyeh has migrated from being a symbol of Palestinian nationalism to being a symbol of Hamas terrorism—which Hamas in turn claims is indeed an expression of Palestinian nationalism.

And so a Westerner wearing a keffiyeh is not only engaging in acts of apparent bigotry, akin to blackfacing, but the act also suggests that Palestinians are defined by terrorism. It is not only akin to painting your face black, but also like acting as if you are a member of a gang or any other racist stereotype anti-black bigots engage in.

There is no doubt that there are Palestinians in Palestine who wear the keffiyeh as a sign of self-expression and not as support for terrorism, but they tend to be influenced by the West. Just as jeans and Yankee baseball caps were brought in from the West to Palestinian towns, so is the modern-day use of the keffiyeh. In other words, the Western pro-Palestinian movement has taken over the organic culture of Palestinians on the ground.

To underscore how detached Palestinians are from the keffiyeh, we can look at the events of the Madrid Conference which preceded the Oslo process which shaped modern-day Palestinians. When the Palestine delegation came to the Madrid conference in 1991 to begin a process that later turned into the establishment of the Palestinian Authority, Palestinians were reportedly angry at one Palestinian delegate (Saeb Erekat) who decided to show up wearing a keffiyeh draped around his shoulders. This is 1991 and the world should not think of Palestinians in terms of wandering Arabs from the movie *Lawrence of Arabia*, the thinking went, because the delegation was attempting to form a national movement. The Palestinian delegation was careful not to allow Western opponents to stereotype them and demean them through symbols of the past.

Moreover, the type of keffiyeh seen at "pro-Palestine" demonstrations supports the claim made by some that Palestine is an "invented nation" (as expressed by Newt Gingrich, for one), and that the idea of a "second" Palestinian state is ludicrous since there already is a Palestinian state—Jordan. The red keffiyeh seen in pro-Palestinian demonstrations is the symbol of the Hashemite Kingdom of Jordan, implying that Palestinians are really part of Jordan, not of Palestine.

Until 1988, Jordan itself held that there was no such thing as a Palestinian nation. It claimed that the West Bank that Israel holds and where Palestinians reside, should be part of Jordan. This stance ended in 1988 in a speech by King Hussein. Jordan today no longer holds claims to the West Bank and now supports the Palestinian cause. So here come Western pro-Palestinian demonstrators and with the keffiyeh echoing what Newt Gingrich and other conservative thinkers have often stated: "Jordan is Palestine."

By wearing the keffiyeh, the symbol of the Western pro-Palestinian movement, those Westerners risk not only being perceived as Islamophobic and racist, but also as anti-Palestinian.

EUROPEAN OCCUPATION OF PALESTINE

Some Palestinians refer to the "Triple Occupation" of Palestine—by Israel, by the Palestinian Authority, and by the Europeans. Many Palestinians view the Palestinian Authority as a corrupt entity composed of outside invaders and some still refer to the PA as "The Tunisians." The Europeans occupy the Palestinian mind and spirit by creating Palestinian dependencies on both Europe and conflict perpetuation. Europe along with Western pro-Palestinians successfully reduced Palestinianism to a single issue—the occupation.

A resident of Bethlehem once told me a joke: If you tell your neighbor in Bethlehem that your car did not start this morning, you will notice the menacing shadow of an EU official creeping up behind you. He will correct you—your car did not start this morning…because of the occupation."

Europe is the occupier of the Palestinian mind, its development, and its true character, and Western pro-Palestinians are willing accomplices in this occupation. Besides cruelly blocking Palestinian employment and mentorship in Jewish-owned businesses, Europeans exploit the Palestinians by creating debilitating dependencies on the conflict and on Europe. In addition, the Palestinian Authority's budget is dependent on conflict-related grants. The end of the conflict could mean the end of Palestinianism. The core merits of the Israeli-Arab feud may not be as deep as that of other conflicts, such as the Spanish-Catalan, Italian-Tyrolean, and the growing European-Islam conflict. Yet, it is hyperpolarized to the tune of billions of euros.

DEHUMANIZATION OF PALESTINIANS

As discussed, while civilians in war zones who wish to flee do so, including Israelis in the north and south of Israel. The people of Gaza cannot. The U.S. and the West apparently chose not to use their leverage over Egypt to craft safe passageways out for the over a million Gazans refugees, many wishing to leave through Egypt to third-world countries.

What do many of those refugees want? to leave. What do pro-Palestinians want? For them to stay.

The misery of the Gazans is of paramount interest to the western pro-Palestinian movement. Some believe that there are others who do not allow Palestinians to leave Gaza, like those promoting the idea of the two-state solution—a sacrosanct Western idea rejected by Israelis and Palestinians alike. After all, for a Palestinian state to exist, it needs Palestinians. If Gazans flee, it will sabotage the idea of the two-state solution.

Either way, if Western pro-Palestinians truly cared about Palestinians, they would pressure their governments to help those Palestinians wishing to flee Gaza. Instead, they bash Israel.

The assault on Judaism through the Western pro-Palestinian movement is counter-woke and counter-DEI. It dehumanizes Palestinians and suppresses their freedom of employment, consumption, and residence. It denies them the basic human right of personal self-determination. The Western pro-Palestinian movement is perhaps today's most profound expression of Western colonialism

This should come as no surprise since the roots of the 2020s Western "pro-Palestinian" colonialism are intertwined with the "pro-Palestinian" colonialism of the 1920s.

THE 1920 PROJECT

The Middle East was peaceful in 1920. There was high optimism as an organic "two-state solution" was taking shape: a Jewish state in the making in Palestine (consisting of today's Israel, the West Bank, and parts of Jordan), living next to a pro-Zionist Arab kingdom in Syria.

The Hashemite Arab Kingdom of Syria was led by King Faisal, who was the consensus Arab leader of the region. Not only was Faisal a Zionist, but he also lobbied the world powers for the establishment of a Jewish homeland in Palestine, stating that clearly in the 1919 Paris Peace Conference. He made his unequivocal support for Zionism no secret.

The British were aware of the broad Arab support for Faisal in Palestine and the region but wanted to verify that Arabs in the region held similar pro-Zionist views as their king. They tasked T.E. Lawrence—Lawrence of Arabia—with checking Arab sentiments toward Zionism. As British Prime Minister David Lloyd

George recounted in his memoirs, Lawrence confirmed that Zionism indeed had broad Arab support.

When founding the Zionist moment in 1897, Theodore Herzl understood that Zionism worked in unison with the interest of the local Arabs. He himself researched the Arab stance and in his 1902 novel *AltNeuLand*, which describes life in a future Jewish state, a Muslim is one of the leaders of the Jewish state. Yet Herzl, who died in 1904, also predicted something else: Europe would never leave the Jews alone. He warned that European animosity would follow the Jews to the Jewish state. As discussed, he wrote in 1895, "In the first 25 years of our existence we need, for our development, some rest from Europe, its wars and social complications." Stunningly, exactly twenty-five years after Herzl wrote this, Europe ended its "rest" and exported its cherished obsession with war to the Middle East.

European Disruptive Intervention Begins

France was the first to export the European obsession of war to the Middle East. It invaded the nascent Arab kingdom in 1920, ending the trajectory toward the Herzl-envisioned peaceful Middle East. France argued that the Arab land of Syria belonged to them. This was not based on a historic connection of the French people to Syria, but on an agreement between a mid-level French foreign-office official named Francois Picot and the British diplomat Mark Sykes—the same Mark Sykes who along with Lawrence shaped today's Middle East in line with the interests of British colonialism. Sykes even designed the flag that a century later is waved in pro-Palestinian demonstrations in Europe and the United States.

France's invasion of Syria led to the removal of the Arab monarch from Syria. To compensate the Hashemite Arab king of Syria, the British carved Palestine into two (along with giving Iraq to his Hashemite family). Indeed, it was due to the French aggression, that the British had to reduce their vision of the "two-state solution," to use our contemporary term, from a Jewish state in Palestine living side by side next to an Arab kingdom in Syria—to a Jewish state in half of Palestine (west of the Jordan river) living next to an Arab Hashemite kingdom in the other half of Palestine (east of the Jordan river).

Indeed, this territory, once promised to the Jews, is today the Hashemite Kingdom of Jordan, which just like its Syrian predecessor, is an ally of the Jewish state.

That same French invasion also led to the 1920 Tel Chai events—the first shots in what later became known as the Israeli-Palestinian conflict: Local Arab Bedouin fighting the French, suspected that the Jews of Tel Chai were hiding French soldiers. In what some historians attribute to a series of misunderstandings, fighting ensued and eight Jews were killed, including iconic Zionist activist Yosef Trumpeldor, to whom the saying "It is good to die for our country" is attributed.

Palestinians Never Wanted to Be Palestinians

The takeover of Syria from France created the making of textbook woke and DEI story: Arabs living in peace and optimism, which is violated by invaders from Europe, who then force them out of their county, use them to promote their own European objectives, and then coerce a new identity on them. That identity later shapes a century of Western narrative when it comes to the Middle East, and is the nucleus of the contemporary western assault on Judaism.

Indeed, there are parallels between the 1619 project (the book and series) and the 1920 project. Palestine might have been a desolate land with a sparse population as described by Mark Twain and other 19th century travelers, but it was certainly not without people. There were Bedouin, Arab Fellahin farming their lands, and an Arab urban population in both Arab cities and mixed cities, such as Jerusalem—where Jews were the majority—and in Hebron, Jaffa, and Gaza—where Arabs were the majority.

It would be an exaggeration to say that there was a national sentiment among Arab in Palestine, but those who did develop such sentiment expressed that Arab nationalism naturally in terms of Syrian nationalism.

In it important to underscore that Arab nationalism in Palestine in the 1920s was Syrian. No Arab in Palestine back then would say he was a "Palestinian." Some would say they are Syrian, but most would just say they were from Nablus or Jerusalem, or this clan or the other—or maybe simply say they are Arab. Western nationalism had not yet been imported to the Middle East, but the actions of Mark Sykes and T. E Lawrence, as well as the establishment of the Syrian Arab Kingdom, gave rise to the early traces of nationalism. That nationalism of the Arabs in Palestine was unequivocally Syrian.

That made sense. There was an Arab king who had the support and admiration of the locals, whether expressed in terms of Syrian nationalism or just loyalty. In came European Colonialists who forced the Arabs to stop identifying as Syrian. From now on, white colonialists told them, you will refer to yourself in this new term we invented for you: Palestinians!

Arabs in Palestine wanted to be Syrian. European Colonists wanted them to be Palestinians. Guess who won?

Fast forward one hundred years, and guess who is waving the flag that would have been so offensive to Arabs in Palestine in 1920?

What happened between the "1920 project" and the "2024 project"? The answer is more European abuse of Palestinian Arabs. The European-forced "rewiring" of Arabs into Palestinians, as if they were just a resource of Western colonialists, was just the beginning. As discussed, the British, who were given a mandate by the League of Nations that included ushering in a Jewish homeland in Palestine, reneged on their mandate. They decided instead to treat Palestine as one of their colonies and deployed colonialist ruling tactics. A key tactic throughout British colonies was "divide and rule"—incite one group against the other.

That is exactly what the British began doing in Palestine. They promoted the most radical elements in Palestinian Arab society, such as Amin al-Husseini. They looked the other way when those radicals eliminated their more moderate Arab rivals, and through a series of what could be viewed as either deliberate or ignorant moves facilitated the breakout of the first large-scale Arab attacks on Jews in 1929.

As Europe was ready to go to war (again), Germany identified the Palestinian Arabs as a resource against the British. They elevated nationalist sentiments and deployed German nationalism invocation mechanisms of that time (such as youth movements.) This led to the Arab uprising of the 1930s, which arguably contributed to the British decision to abandon their "colony" a decade later in 1948. It is ironic that Husseini, who the British nurtured and promoted upon taking control of their Palestine "colony" was in Germany twenty years later, strategizing against the British.

Up until then, Western exploitation of Palestinians was done in accordance with organic European intents: The French wanted Syria and the British used them as a counterweight to their Jewish "competitors." (The British were tasked with building a homeland for the Jews, but wanted Palestine for themselves), and the Germans used them as a counterforce to the British. Starting in 1993, the Western exploitation of the Palestinians was done in the context of the Western assault on Judaism.

Indeed, the 1920 project—the Western exploitation of Palestinians—continued in 1993 with the aftermath of the Oslo Accords and the creation of the Conflict-Industry, which reduced anything and everything that is Palestinian to a single issue, "the occupation," so much that if the occupation ended, "Palestinianism" would likely end.

Herzl and Zionism to the Rescue of Palestinians?

Perhaps it is time for Palestinians to rebel against their Europeans and Western pro-Palestinian colonialist oppressors, go back to their roots, and support Zionism?

The big secret: Many do!

This is where the Palestinians can rely on Herzl. The father of Zionism viewed the Jewish realities of his time (Judaism 2.0) as a reaction to European persecution. So dominant were those centuries of persecution—deportations, limits on Jewish professionals, on how many children they could have, incarceration in Jewish ghettos—that they defined the Jewish nation and hence united it. Yet, once the Jews returned home and those European antisemitic pressures that united them no longer existed, what would become of the Jews?

Herzl answered that in an 1894 criticism of Alexandre Dumas's play *The Wife of Claude*, in which the Jews return to their land: "They would discover the very next morning that they long ago ceased to be one people," Herzl concluded. Therefore, there was a need to replace the uniting feature of European persecution that "made Jews of us," to use Herzl's words, with an ideological, political, and diplomatic infrastructure of Judaism.

That is Zionism.

Indeed, Zionism for Herzl is organic Judaism (Judaism 3.0), as opposed to the Judaism of his time, which was a reactionary Judaism, a Judaism based on European persecution (Judaism 2.0). Zionism was a return to a time when Jews were not only in their own land but were free (Judaism 1.0).

Similarly, for Palestinians, it is Europeans and Western pro-Palestinians who have made "the Occupation" the only issue that unites Palestinians. What if one day there was a State of Palestine and the occupation that unites them ended? Applying Herzl's thinking, Palestinians too might "discover the very next morning that they long ago ceased to be one people."

A true national movement that is self-sustaining needs to be organic, and not exclusively based on an external force that, once gone, ends the national movement.

Let's have no illusions, the Palestinians are a valuable resource in the assault on Judaism, including through the structure of the Western pro-Palestinian colonialist movement. The idea of the "end of occupation" or establishment of a "State of Palestine" runs contrary to their raison d'être, and given that they are the ones with the means and power, they would never let Palestinians achieve that.

Waving the Flag of Colonialism

Mark Sykes designed the Palestinian flag as part of the plan to draft the Arab tribes in today's Saudi Arabia and throughout the Middle East for the British war against the Ottomans. Just as Herzl learned from Bismark that "with a flag one can lead men wherever one wants to," so too did Mark Sykes and the British colonialists. They used a flag to draft the local Arab population and promote British interests.

That flag became the symbol for the Arabs fighting for the British against the Muslim Ottomans. It was later adopted by various Arab countries resulting from the European meddling in the Middle East. It is ironic that in their assault on Judaism, Western pro-Palestinian colonialists use the flag created by British colonialism.

Lawrence of Arabia: "Outright immoral"

European exploitation of Palestinians and other Middle Eastern Arabs has lasted for over a century.

T. E. Lawrence, who instigated the 1916 Arab Revolt, reflected in his later years that what he did was "outright immoral." At the time though, it seems he really believed that he was supporting the Arab cause and was doing the right thing.

Will Western "pro-Palestinians" who today truly believe that they are doing the right thing, reach the same conclusion as Lawrence of Arabia—that what they are doing to the Palestinians is utterly immoral? If at least some of those pro-Palestinians reach this inevitable conclusion, it would encourage them to find another cause, more in line with progressive values and DEI objectives, as opposed to a cause that promotes colonialism, Islamophobia, and the suppression of the Palestinian people.

I have seen it happen over the years, with members of the conflict-industry—those coming to Jerusalem to work for UNRWA, or one of the other UN agencies, for NGOs, and for the EU. Most of them come with good intentions. I have known many of them over the years and even admired their conviction to leave everything behind to support a cause that they truly believe helps humanity. Some of them realize after some time, just like Lawrence of Arabia, that what they are doing is "outright immoral."

Conversations with people who reach this conclusion could be a topic of a whole different book, but if people who made a career of (inadvertently) exploiting the Palestinians can change, then Western pro-Palestinians can come to understand the consequences of their actions and realize that they are the oppressors of the Palestinians, that they are the colonialists.

CHAPTER 12

RECOGNIZE THE OBVIOUS: ZIONISM BECAME THE ANCHOR OF JUDAISM

A necessary condition for Israel-basher-lites to carry on the assault on Judaism is their perceived separation of Judaism from Zionism. For them, Zionism, the national aspect of the Jewish nation-religion, is not the same as Judaism, which for many of them is reduced to mean the religious and cultural aspect of the Jewish nation-religion. Therefore, according to this logic, being anti-Zionist is not the same as being anti-Jewish, and certainly accusing the Jewish state of hideous behavior is not the same as accusing Jews of that hideous behavior.

Israel-basher-lites must stay in the legacy version of Judaism (Judaism 2.0)—the Judaism of two thousand years of exile, anchored in strong religiosity on the inside and complete insularity on the outside—neither of which reflect today's Jewish realities.

As the religious connecter of the Jewish nation-religion eroded, the national connector was dramatically augmented: The Jewish state was reestablished in 1948, and after nearly eighty years, it is evident that Judaism is transforming and Zionism is becoming its anchor. Whether positive or negative, both Jews and non-Jews relate to Judaism today primarily through the prism of Zionism and the Jewish state—Judaism 3.0. (For more on that, see Judaism-Zionism.com.)

This relates to a key common characteristic of the Israel-basher lite. No matter what he may think of Judaism or the Jews, he cannot afford the risk of being perceived as an antisemite. If deemed a Jew-basher, he could lose his job and become a social outcast. For most, this would also carry a dire emotional price—being perceived as an antisemite would deeply offend them (especially if they are Jewish themselves).

Israel-basher-lites have a lot to lose and therefore tend to be risk-averse. Unlike the hard-core Israel-basher who operates in the extremes and can sustain being labeled as a Jew-hater, the Israel-basher-lite operates in the middle and refrains from taking actions or making statements that can lead people to think that he is an antisemite.

When the Israel-basher-lite participates in imposing sanctions on Israeli Jews, he does not view it as an anti-Jewish action, since he does not sanction those who engage in circumcision or keep Shabbat. When he singles out Israel for condemnation, he does not engage in anti-Jewish activity since he does not condemn the Jewish holidays or keeping Kosher. He is not anti-Jewish, because Judaism to him is a religion.

His assault on Judaism is done through a sword and a shield. The sword is Israel-bashing, and the shield is Judaism 2.0—the illusion that Judaism is anchored in its religious aspect, and therefore Israel-bashing is not Jew-bashing, and anti-Zionism is not anti-Judaism.

The path-of-destruction of Judaism can only continue past him if he can reassure himself that he is not attacking Judaism. Indeed, many of the Israel-basher-lites are at the forefront of those chanting "zero tolerance for antisemitism." To demonstrate that, many make it a point to visit Holocaust remembrance museums such as Yad Vashem and speak about the horrors of the Holocaust.

Israel-basher-lites' strong stance of zero-tolerance for antisemitism (the threat to Judaism in the 20th century) serves as a "Kosher-certificate" for partaking in Israel-bashing (the threat to Judaism in the 21st century.) Similarly, many of them celebrate features of 20th-century Judaism, such as eating Gefilte fish, watching *Fiddler on the Roof*, or using Yiddish words. This gives them self-legitimacy to engage in Israel-bashing, while being assured by their echo chamber that their actions do not amount to antisemitism.

ANTISEMITISM TURNS INTO AN ASSET

The battle to save Judaism has a not-so-obvious secret weapon: antisemitism itself. Unlike in previous large-scale assaults on Judaism, in this era's assault, it is taboo to say in the West, "I hate Jews." Therefore, one needs to direct opposition to Jews through Zionism and the Jewish state as in "I am not anti-Jewish, I am only anti-Zionist."

Once there is a global recognition that Judaism has transformed and Zionism is now its anchor (Judaism 3.0), that false facade is shattered. Such recognition would turn the Israel-basher into a Jew-basher, and this would alter the nature of the threat:

The Israel-basher-lite has too much to lose to be perceived as such, and therefore he would be deterred from attacking.

As mentioned, a prerequisite for the Israel-basher-lites' attack on Judaism through Zionism is the possession of the shield of Judaism 2.0. But that shield only exists in their bubble among their narrow milieu. Gradually, more and more of them are learning just how detached their views are relative to how the broader world views Judaism.

This was the subject of conversations and briefings I had in the summer of 2024 in Washington, New York, and throughout the U.S. in connection with the release of a new edition of my 2022 book *Judaism 3.0: Judaism's Transformation to Zionism*, updated for the Gaza war. Just as Herzl had friends and acquaintances in the late 19th century that were antisemites, I have friends who are Israel-basher-lites—in government, media, academia, multinational organizations, as well as amongst Democratic party funders. To their credit, many of them engaged with the ideas of Judaism 3.0, quite a few read the book, and some wanted to know to what degree there is such global awareness that Judaism transformed and Zionism is now its anchor.

My answer was clear: October 7th removed any lingering doubt that we are in Judaism 3.0.

IT IS EVIDENT THAT WE ARE IN JUDAISM 3.0

A Jewish student on a college campus in the spring of 2024 felt that he was in Judaism 3.0 on a day-to-day basis. His Jewish affiliation was dominated by his affiliation with Israel. The same went for the broader American Jewish community, European Jews, and Jews around the world. No other Jewish issue has taken so much of the Jew's headspace as Israel. It was not a choice one made. It was a reality imposed on Jews, whether they liked it or not.

They were viewed through the prism of Zionism. Just as Herzl predicted, it is Zionism that has returned Jews to their Judaism.

This was true for engaged Jews, and this was true for unaffiliated Jews. Visiting Harvard, one graduate student told me he stopped taking buses in Boston, since he felt accusatory looks from passengers due to his Jewish appearance. A Jewish high-school junior applying to top-notch universities explained she is now considering Israeli universities, since she feels unwelcome on American college campuses. Such sense of unwelcome was due to her passive affiliation with Zionism, which exists merely due to having a Jewish last name. Indeed, an initiative was launched in the summer of 2024 to facilitate American Jewish student enrollment in Israeli universities instead of American universities.

The American Jew's connection to Judaism through Zionism certainly does not mean that he thinks about Israel regularly. It means that when he thinks of Judaism, fears of Judaism, or engages with Judaism, it is mostly through Israel.

This, in part, is because other aspects of Judaism are becoming less and less relevant in the life of most American Jews.

American Jews Connect to Judaism via Zionism

With the exception of the Orthodox (less than 10 percent of American Jewry), Judaism is by now low on the hierarchy of identities for most American Jews and inferior to other identities—such as alumni identity, professional identity, and gender identity. The Jew might go about his day-to-day life without encountering much of his Jewishness. That is with one exception—Zionism pulls him back into Judaism, whether he likes it or not.

At the same time, Zionism provides an organic connection to Judaism that is initiated by the Jew himself as opposed to a reluctant connection made due to guilt or duty. This is both in the negative, such as criticizing Israel, and in the positive, such as consuming Israeli wine. There is a cultural Israelization of the American-Jewish experience. Israeli cuisine is replacing old Jewish food such as gefilte fish, while Israeli music, TV shows, icons, news, and vibrancy are replacing connection through the Holocaust, Yiddish, and the Jewish past. In addition, many American Jews feel a connection to Judaism through the value of Tikkun Olam—repairing the world. This value is now best expressed through the Jewish state. From increasing longevity of the world's population through medical innovations to ending famine by turning air into water, Israel has become the Tikkun Olam state, and Zionism has become a "light to the nations."

Israelis Connect to Judaism via Zionism

The realities of Judaism 3.0 in America are complemented by those in Israel, where Zionism has long been the primary vehicle that connects Jews to their Judaism. It is the uniting ideology for all Israeli Jews—secular, religious, and Ultra-Orthodox, who contribute to Israeli Zionist society in their own way, such as through volunteering as motorcycle medics who save hundreds of Israeli lives each year.

A little taste of that was seen on June 8, 2024. On that day, Israeli forces rescued four hostages in a heroic military raid in Gaza. Lifeguards on the beaches of Tel Aviv announced the good news on loudspeakers to the cheers of the crowds.

It was Saturday, the Jewish Sabbath—just as on October 7th—when religious people do not check their phones or watch TV. Therefore secular Israelis knocked on their religious neighbors' doors and placed notes on Synagogue doors to tell worshipers the good news, and then they prayed to thank God.

Spontaneous celebrations erupted on the streets of Tel Aviv and cities throughout Israel. Underscoring the degree to which Israelis—secular and religious alike—are a nation of believers, the two most common popular Israeli songs heard in those spontaneous celebrations of secular Israelis are "He who believes [In God], is not afraid," and "Our father [Israel] is still alive, the nation of Israel is alive."

Indeed, Zionism is the ideological bedrock in which Israeli Jewish society is rooted. There are ample policy debates within Zionism, but not about Zionism. In fact, it is exactly the strength of the Zionist ideal that enables the numerous points of division in Israel to be argued passionately yet safely.

Eight months after the October 7th holiday of Simchat Torah, Jews celebrated the holiday of Shavuot. The sight at 4 a.m. in Jerusalem was hard to describe—thousands of Israeli Jews from all walks of life walking towards the gates of the Old City of Jerusalem, some with Israeli flags and many with songs, and from there proceeding to the Western Wall to participate in the sunrise holiday prayer. The display of joy and resilience, as the Israeli song goes "from eulogy to dance," was the display of the triumph of Zionism. This was certainly a Jewish religious experience—but it was celebrated through a Zionist framing.

Growing Global Awareness That Zionism Is the Anchor of Judaism

The realities of the Jewish transformation are becoming more and more visible to the world. One indication of how broadly acceptable is the idea that Judaism has transformed and that Zionism is now its anchor was evident with the nature of opposition that I have received to my book *Judaism 3.0.*

The pushback was not to the thesis, that Zionism is now the anchor of Judaism, but mostly over the question of whether this is good or bad, as well as disagreement about the implications. Some critics viewed it as alarming that "Zionism is taking over Judaism" or that Judaism is "being corrupted by Zionism." Some even went so far as to say that Judaism is under an existential risk, not due to the attack on Judaism as I argue, but due to "Zionism taking over Judaism." Rarely did I see an article, comment, or letter from readers that disagreed that Zionism was becoming the central feature of Judaism.

Natan Sharansky, the human-right activities and former head of the Jewish Agency, predicted this. He read *Judaism 3.0* before it was published and told me that I have dozens of provocative and original observations in the book. "One will always find something to disagree about," he said, "but the central idea of Judaism 3.0 that Zionism takes the center stage in the broad field of Jewish identity is powerful and is absolutely true."

The Assault on Judaism from Within

Judaism is under an ideological assault from the West alongside a physical assault from Hamas, Iran, and its proxies, but it is also under a more subtle one enabled by 21st century American realities.

While most Americans of Jewish ancestry wish to keep their Jewish affiliation and would defend Judaism vigorously, a small, yet powerful minority welcomes the prospects of ending Judaism. For years, Jews could not get out—now they finally can, but Zionism stands in the way. Similarly, there are those who wish to end Judaism through downgrading it into a "concept" that inspires all people, regardless of their ancestral background. Zionism stands in their way as well, as it is about

Jewish particularity and nationalism. These dynamics, on the one hand, underscore that Zionism has turned into the anchor of Judaism, but on the other incentivize some to engage in obsessive Israel-bashing.

As realities of Judaism 3.0 set it, the nature of such obsessive behavior is becoming clear:

ISRAEL BASHING = JEW-BASHING

Just as we are in the midst of a historic transformation of Judaism today, there was a similar shift in the consciousness of what Judaism is some two thousand years ago. As discussed, after the Jews left Judea they adopted a new organizing principle—Rabbinic Judaism: The synagogues replaced the Temple, the insular ghetto replaced the insular life in Judea, and the ritualistic yearning to return to Zion replaced the actual presence in Jerusalem (Judaism 2.0). After some time, the terms "Rabbinic Judaism" and "Judaism" became synonymous.

It is possible that at that time, some argued they loved the Jews (those who used to worship in the Temple and live in Judea) but hated the Jews in the European ghettos (those who worship in synagogues, wear a kippah, and celebrate Purim and Hanukkah). Once there was a global recognition that Judaism had transformed into Judaism 2.0, one could not hide behind this facade.

Similarly, once there is a global recognition that we are in Judaism 3.0, one will not be able to hide behind the facade of loving the Jews who (used to) go to synagogue and speak Yiddish, but hating the Zionists. In such a reality, once it is clear that we are in Judaism 3.0, those in government and the media who partake in the assault on Judaism would be less likely to attack.

That BBC reporter would not want to be perceived as saying that "Jews love killing children." Senator Schumer would not want to be perceived as saying that Jews are pariahs opposed by the rest of the world, and Secretary Blinken would not want to be perceived as implying that Jews poison the wells of humanity, just as President Trudeau would not want to be perceived as saying that Jews kill women, children, and babies.

They can make their statements now because of the false perception that the world is in Judaism 2.0. Once they internalize that Judaism has transformed, they would be deterred from slandering the Jewish state. Unlike hard-core Israel-bashers, the Israel-basher-lites have a lot to lose: their position, their office, and most of all, their reputation and legacy.

This has a trickle-down effect. Just as there were hundreds of Babylonian soldiers and administrators who were planning the physical siege of Jerusalem—a siege that eventually led to the destruction of Jerusalem and expulsion of Jews—there are today hundreds of low, mid, and high-level bureaucrats planning the economic siege of Jerusalem—a siege, that, as discussed, is a building block in the attempt to eradicate Judaism.

Those are not organic antisemites. Most of them are admirable people who chose to serve the public and are driven by doing the right thing. Once they realize that Judaism has transformed and Zionism is now its anchor, they will come on their own to the inevitable conclusion that their partaking in the siege of Zion is the same as their partaking in the siege of Judaism—an attempt to eradicate Judaism.

In the 1890s, Mayor Karl Lueger of Vienna was faced with critics who chided him for openly advocating antisemitism, while he had Jewish friends. He had a simple answer: "I will decide who is Jewish." Yet, over time it was clear that his definition of "who is Jewish" was detached from that of the outside world. Indeed,

Lueger is remembered as an antisemite, as a Jew-hater, and for the right reason—he was!

The Israel-basher-lites today still feel they can "decide what is Judaism." They can vigorously defend the anchor of Judaism 2.0 (the religious aspects and exile culture), and at the same time vigorously attack the anchor of Judaism 3.0 (Zionism and by extension, the Jewish state). As it becomes clear that Judaism has transformed, their ability to "decide what is Judaism" is getting diminished.

Unlike Lueger who did not care if he was perceived as an antisemite, they do. As discussed, they are risk-averse and would refrain from doing anything that could raise questions and sabotage their career and legacy. Even for those Israel-basher-lites who are not convinced, and for whom it did not yet resonate fully that Zionism has become the anchor of Judaism, their risk-aversion could deter them for carrying on with their assault.

This is especially after witnessing a powerful Judaism 3.0 "case study" that was near and dear to their hearts.

The Josh Shapiro VP Consideration Showed That We Are in Judaism 3.0

During the summer of 2024, I spent time with journalists covering the race to the White House, and was with them at the August 6th Kamala Harris Philadelphia rally where she unveiled her running mate.

As of a few days prior, those journalists, as well as Democrat party insiders, said that Harris had chosen Pennsylvania Governor Josh Shapiro as her vice president candidate. But Shapiro was not the one picked, and that, according to the consensus amongst the pundits, was for one reason: He is Jewish.

Shapiro's positions on Israel are not much different from those of Tim Walz, the VP pick, and other Democrat politicians.

Similarly, Shapiro was the one to get the title "Genocide Josh," while non-Jewish supporters of Israel did not.

"This is not a time for a Jewish person on the ticket," a prominent Democratic politician told me privately, while others echoed similar sentiments: Having a Jewish vice president candidate is just not palatable in the current environment.

Even though Shapiro is a practicing Jew, for the American electorate, his Judaism meant one thing and one thing only— association with Israel.

This "Judaism 3.0 message" on something that matters so much was received loud and clear—by those in the Treasury and State Department holding the "license to sanction" Israeli Jews, by those considering making speeches on the Senate floors about the Jewish state being a "pariah opposed by the rest of the world," and by my fellow journalists in the press box. We are in Judaism 3.0—Jews are viewed through the prism of Zionism, and therefore Israel-bashing = Jew-bashing.

Indeed, while the path to eradicate Judaism is disrupted on the hard-core Israel-bashers level by their fear that their actions could be perceived as colonialist and counter-DEI (as they really are), the path to eradicate Judaism is disrupted on the Israel-basher-lites' level through their fear that their actions could be deemed antisemitic (as they really are).

These disruptions are long-term processes that take time to develop but could eventually provide a sustainable protective shield against the assault on Judaism. However, we are already far down the path to eradicating Judaism, and there is also a need for an immediate response.

The assault on Judaism does not only threaten the Jews and the Jewish state; it also threatens the global power that has the capabilities to disrupt the path to destruction of Judaism.

CHAPTER 13

GLOBAL LEADERSHIP: AN ATTACK ON AMERICANISM

When President John F. Kennedy met Israeli Prime Minister David Ben-Gurion in May 1961, a few months after taking office, Kennedy told Ben-Gurion: "I know I got elected thanks to the Jewish vote. I owe them my election."

Kennedy wanted to reward Ben-Gurion and the Jewish state for that. As Ben-Gurion biographer Michael Bar Zohar recounted, he asked Ben-Gurion, "Tell me, is there anything I should do?" Ben-Gurion answered, "You should do what is best for the free world." This underscores a key principle of Israel's strategic doctrine: The prime interest of the Jewish state is a strong America. At no time has this been more the case than today, as the assault on Judaism unfolds.

The assault on Judaism is not just a threat to the Jewish nation, it is a threat to America and the stability of the free world. The threat to America is both at the short-term practical level and the long-term strategic level. From a practical point of view, the assault paves the way for the ICC to arrest Americans and trigger global instability: "Globalize the Intifada."

From a long-term strategic point of view, the assault on Judaism is an assault on the essence of Americanism and an attempt to negate the values of the American Revolution. After all, America was founded on Judeo-Christian values, and in contrast to prevailing European dogmas, such as using Judaism and Jews as a target to address European frustrations. Moreover, the assault on the Jewish state is in many respects a proxy for an assault on the United States of America.

IMMINENT THREAT TO AMERICA

The threat to America does not lie in the risk that Judaism will be eradicated (spoiler alert: Judaism will survive the assault), but rather in the "journey." It is the path to eradicating Judaism that poses a potent threat to America.

The International Criminal Court

Indeed, the path-of-destruction of Judaism goes through the International Criminal Court. When its prosecutor announced that he was seeking to issue arrest warrants for Israel's prime minister and defense minister, it opened the door to issuing such warrants for the president of the United States and the secretary of defense. When the ICC implies it might do the same for Israeli soldiers, it opens the door to issuing such warrants for American soldiers. This is not a hypothetical. The ICC has already tried to investigate the United States. Back in 2020, President Donald Trump responded swiftly with strong sanctions.

American and Western military experts call Israel the most moral army in the world. Israeli tactics are far more civilian-sensitive than other armies. Israel takes extreme measures to protect the lives of uninvolved civilians—at times, at a heavy operational cost. For example, "knocking on the roof"—a unique tactic Israel has been using for years to warn a terrorist of an incoming air bombing, allows uninvolved civilians (such as the terrorist's family) to escape to safety, but it also allows the terrorist himself to escape, along with military assets that later will be used to kill Israeli soldiers and civilians. It is clearly an ineffective tool when it comes to warfare and can inevitably lead to Israeli casualties, but it is in line with the high moral bar that Israel sets for itself. Colonel Richard Kemp, former commander of the British Forces in Afghanistan and Iraq, has testified that: "The IDF is the most moral army in the history of warfare." Similarly, Col. John Spencer, chair of urban warfare studies at the Modern War Institute at West Point, wrote in a March 25, 2024 *Newsweek* article that Israel set a "historic new standard" for urban warfare: "In my long career studying and advising on urban warfare for the U.S. military, I've never known an army to take such measures to attend to the enemy's civilian population."

If political leaders and soldiers of the most moral army in the world get indicted for war crimes by the ICC for the way they fight, then certainly leaders and soldiers of armies a notch below could. This is especially true in a legal system based on precedents in which the ICC operates.

President George W. Bush estimated in 2005 that about thirty thousand Iraqi civilians died in the Iraq War. As the war progressed, some estimates put total casualty numbers anywhere between one hundred thousand and six hundred thousand people. That's twenty times the estimated casualties in Gaza. The UN estimated that there were about 4.5 million displaced people in that war (more than twice that of Gaza).

In a February 14, 2024 article in *Foreign Policy*, Professor Barry Posen of MIT compared the civilian deaths in Gaza to those in the U.S.-led campaigns against ISIS forces in Syria and Iraq in 2016. Back then, thousands of civilians died from U.S. fire and from buildings that collapsed due to bombing by U.S. forces and allies. "The devastation of Gaza was inevitable," he concluded. "Urban warfare has always been brutal for civilians, and the war against Hamas was designed by the terror group to be an extreme case."

The risk to the U.S. is not just of arrests, but also the fear of arrests. Every time a current or former president goes abroad, there is an enormous amount of security coordination and planning. The assault on Judaism adds to that the fear of an arrest. The same is true for the current and former defense secretary, as set by the ICC precedent. This can trickle down to U.S. military officers and soldiers who do not enjoy the advanced coordination and intelligence gathering that occur when a former president is about to travel to Europe. Therefore, the assault on Judaism can lead to surprise arrests of U.S. military personnel.

European countries can even rationalize arrests of Americans by arguing that the United States did not immediately sanction the ICC for its attempt to arrest Israeli political leaders, and therefore gave its implicit agreement to such actions. Arrest warrants can also come from individual European countries—say if a U.S. soldier was involved in a battle in Iraq that killed a civilian who held European citizenship. (This is arguably supported by the U.S.-planned actions against Netzah Yehuda described in Chapter 8).

It can also lead to demoralization—not only of veterans but also of U.S. troops on the battlefield who know that there is someone in the Netherlands, who, once they come back home safely and dare take a trip to Europe, might be eager to arrest them.

Would this lead to risk-aversion among commanders and fighters on the battlefield, and therefore increase U.S. casualties? If hesitation to shoot the enemy turns into ICC-generated paralysis, this ultimately undermines the ability to prevail in battle. The assault on Judaism could compromise the American military's ability to fight and win.

On May 28, 2024, South Africa's foreign minister revealed that her country is planning to do exactly that: The U.S. is next, she said.

She referenced House of Representative Speaker Mike Johnson's warning that "if the ICC is allowed to threaten Israel's leaders, then we know America will be next." She read his warning and then declared, "Our response is: Of course!"

South Africa has announced its plans to go after the United States, using the ICC, and other legal means. Yet, this is not an organic attack on the United States. This attack was triggered by South Africa's leadership role in the assault on Judaism. In other words, it is the assault on Judaism, per the apparent South African policy, that leads to an assault on the United States of America.

Israel Used as a Proxy for America

More broadly, it is clear that the assault on the Jewish state is a proxy for the assault on America. Iran called America "Big Satan" and Israel "Little Satan." Since Iran is limited in its ability to attack America, it attacks Israel. In other words, Iran attacks America by attacking Israel.

If Israel is the "little war criminal," America is the "big war criminal." If Israeli soldiers are "little dehumanizers," then American soldiers are "big dehumanizers."

It is clear that eventually the forces targeting the Jewish state—whether they use the UN, ICC, European governments, other governments such as South Africa, or multinational organizations—will eventually target America. Therefore, it is in the vital American interest to stop the attack at its current stage—on the Jewish state—before it gets to America. This is not just protecting an ally, this is protecting America.

The assault on America that is coming through the assault on Judaism is both direct—as indicated by the threat issued by South Africa—and indirect, through the global instability that the assault on Judaism generates.

THE ASSAULT ON JUDAISM DESTABILIZES THE WORLD

The Israel-bashing and anti-Zionism ideology is expanding well beyond Israel and Zionism. In assessing global threats for 2025 and beyond, Israel-bashing should be at the top of the list.

Israel-bashers are not keeping their expansion plans a secret: right next to the banners "From the River to the Sea" are the banners "Globalize the Intifada."

Since October 7th, the Israel-bashing and anti-Zionism movement has triggered a series of "global" conversations that have nothing to do with Zionism or Israel. These include Muslim rights in Europe, their perceived suppression by Europeans, and even planting the seeds for a Muslim national movement in Europe. It also led to conversations about defunding universities and a debate about whether universities are even needed anymore, as well as to disruptions of the educational system. Those conversations have nothing to do with Judaism or Israel, but they were triggered as "collateral damage" by those assaulting Judaism.

The 2023–2024 assault on Judaism even reversed a century of progress for women's rights by placing some degree of "context" on rape. The Gaza war gave the Israel-bashing movement momentum, structure, funding, and legitimacy from credible media outlets and politicians. That credibility and capital has since been deployed to the "globalization arm." By energizing the crowd against the "Little War Criminal," the infrastructure, resources, and energy have been set for the upcoming battle against the "Big War Criminal."

Destabilizing the World—Physically

The 2022 riots in France, during which over five thousand cars were burned and one thousand buildings damaged, had nothing to do with Israel either and certainly were not part of the assault on Judaism.

The riots did not "happen in a vacuum," to use UN Secretary-General António Guterres's terminology about the Hamas massacre, and can be viewed as a round in the growing Muslim-Europe tensions.

Then came October 7th, which led to the funding and organization of the assault on Judaism, along with the maturing of Israel-bashing ideology. Now that there is a well-funded, well-organized operation, there is the temptation to "acquire" the next French riots under its "Globalize the Intifada" umbrella. Moreover, it can even be an "acquisition" in retrospect—perhaps the 2022 riots did not happen in a vacuum—it was "the genocide of Palestine" that led Muslims to burn five thousand cars in France.

When one enters a merger and acquisition transaction, it is intended to serve the interests of all sides. This is certainly the case in the assault on Judaism "acquiring" the unrelated riots in France, through the "Globalize the Intifada" arm. The rioters in France could get money, publicity, infrastructure, organization, access to public relations firms, media experts, and consultants.

It would even benefit France!

It is not politically correct to report that the 2022 riots and similar ones were carried out by "young Muslims." A French media outlet reporting it as such would be deemed racist. But if we can place the "immigrants' frustration" in the context of the "Occupation of Palestine," "the Genocide in Palestine," or the "Ethnic Cleansing of the Palestinians…" Bingo!

The riots could then become about "young Muslims" naturally expressing their frustrations with Israel. It gives France both the legitimacy to focus on the perpetrators it is facing (young Muslims), as well as to deflect from the real reason for such riots by insisting that they are not against France, they are against Israel.

In other words, they could say "they are not rioting because a French police officer shot a Muslim youth in France, they are rioting because the Israeli army is committing genocide of Muslims in Palestine. They are not rioting because four armed French police officers approached an unsuspecting Muslim woman on a beach and ordered her to take her top off, they are rioting because the Jews in Israel dehumanize Muslims in Palestine."

What do you expect? Of course, the 2022 riots in France broke out; they were a natural reaction to the 2023–2024 Israeli actions in Gaza. And the same would be the case with other riots in Europe, the United States, and elsewhere. Such "retroactive mergers" can encourage more riots and more violence that until now had nothing to do with Israel and Judaism.

The Assault on Judaism is the "big corporate chain store" that is there to take over all the little stores in Europe—riots all over France, riots in Germany, and throughout Europe—indeed, a "Global Intifada!"

The funding that goes into the Israel-bashing coalition accelerated as 2024 progressed. For example, *Politico* reported in May 2024, that George Soros has been a major funder of anti-Israel protests. Soros and other foundations fund the assault on Judaism through organizations that initiate and manage pro-Palestinian demonstrations. Some of those organizations make no secret of their intention, calling for "worldwide escalation."

On May 27, 2024, for example, pro-Palestinian organizations issued a statement demanding to "escalate protests to an open intifada in every capital." The statement was then distributed and shared by student organizations at Harvard, Princeton, the University of Pennsylvania, and other organizations as reported in a May 28, 2024, *Jerusalem Post* article. This underscores the imminent threat the Assault on Judaism represents to the United States. The calls for an intifada were not issued from a cave in Afghanistan or a tunnel in Gaza but from U.S.-based universities. The funding was not provided by shady, secretive foreign sources, but by U.S.-based foundations who comply with U.S. laws.

Indeed, the "Globalize" arm of the assault on Judaism fulfills the plans outlined by South Africa's foreign minister: America is next!

Destabilizing the World—Ideologically

Just as the assault on Judaism has a physical and an ideological component, so does the "Globalize" arm.

Just like in any other large-scale assaults, the attackers need to get rid of hurdles that are in the way. There are various ideological "problems" that would need to be "sacrificed" for the greater goal of the assault on Judaism. For example, the assault on Judaism can destabilize Spain. As discussed, generations of

Spaniards have been taught about the "Reconquista," the process of expelling Spain's Muslim population, who inhabited Spain for eight hundred years. It is largely due to the assault on Judaism that the historical justification for the existence of Spain now gets challenged. If one gives legitimacy to the term "Reconquista," based on a questionable theory that the people who completed the conquest of Spain in the 15th century were somehow related to the people who lived there eight hundred years earlier, then one gives legitimacy to Zionism, which represents a much more historically sound story about a nation coming back to its ancestral homeland. In other words, one can only be anti-Zionist if one is anti-Spanish.

Add to that other unresolved conflicts in Spain, such as the Basque and Catalonia's quest for independence, and suddenly, the assault on Judaism triggered the "Spanish Question," which remained dormant for over five hundred years!

For years, some members of the conflict-industry in Jerusalem have joked that the two-state solution template they have been working on is merely a laboratory experiment for such a construct in Europe. The assault on Judaism can lead to demand for a declaration of a Muslim state in Europe—not by the Muslims, but by Western Israel-bashers who care about European Muslims as much as they care about Palestinian Muslims.

The "Globalize the Intifada" banner is often situated right next to the "From the River to the Sea" banner. One can figure out with simple math what could come next: "From the Atlantic to the Black Sea, Eurostan will be free."

The destabilization of Europe as "collateral damage" in the assault on Judaism is just one reason why the assault on Judaism should be viewed as a national security threat to the United States.

Destabilize America

Indeed, just like in the case of Iran, which recognizes that firing missiles at America/"big Satan" would have far more serious consequences than firing such missiles at its proxy Israel/"little Satan," the same is the case with those funding anti-Israel riots. If they funded violent riots in America under the anti-America banner, they could be investigated for criminal behavior and held accountable. But by funding "legitimate" protests against Israel, under the banner of being pro-Palestinian, and then globalizing them to U.S. cities, they achieve their objective of destabilizing the United States without paying the price for it. This arguably was the case in Washington, DC, on July 24, 2024, where "legitimate" pro-Palestinians protesting Prime Minister Netanyahu's address to a joint session of Congress burned American flags, vandalized national monuments, and defamed the streets of the nation's capital.

The assault on Judaism is a way to "launder" an attempt to destabilize America. The people who are reportedly funding it, are also the ones who have promoted for years the idea that Judaism is not a nation or a religion, but merely a "concept." Just as Israel-bashing has expanded "globally" to target not just the "little war criminal," but also the "big war criminal," so can the term Palestine be expanded from a geography and a group of people to a concept that addresses a range of grievances and frustrations. We saw this, for example, at the University of Pennsylvania's Palestine Writes Festival. If one can use the concept of "Palestine" as an inspiration to write about occupation and human rights violations around the world, one can also use the concept of "Palestine" to destabilize America through seemingly legitimate means.

To illustrate through an extreme example: If someone wanted to promote the preposterous idea of establishing a Muslim Caliphate in Virginia, he would be met with complete rejection and mockery, including from Muslim Americans. But if it was promoted through the indirect channel of funding public relations campaigns, demonstrations, and riots that support the right for the State of Palestine, one could get a much better result. According to the Pew Research Center, Muslims are soon going to be over 2 percent of the American population—why should they be denied equal proportional sovereignty?

Moreover, Turkey's President Tayyip Erdoğan has already introduced the notion that Muslims were the first to arrive in America. According to him, they came over in the 12th century, nearly three hundred years before Columbus. The BBC reported research by the historian Youssef Mroueh, who claims that a diary entry by Columbus "was proof that Muslims had reached the Americas first" and that "the religion of Islam was widespread" in America. Such claims are refuted by historians, but that is no problem. One can donate money to a U.S. university to fund a "Chair for 15th century American Muslim life," so that someone can research the validity of claims of early Muslim life in Virginia, hold conferences, and spread the word.

This, of course, is an extreme example to illustrate that the assault on Judaism provides a path for a two-step assault on America. Yet, such assault is not only carried out through extreme elements; it is coming from the heart of mainstream society.

AN ATTACK ON THE AMERICAN REVOLUTION

Every century has its global philosophical divide. In the 19th century, it was monarchy vs. republic. In the 20th century, it was communism vs. capitalism. This era's philosophical divide may be Europeanism vs. Americanism.

For two thousand years, Europe dominated the world from an economical and military point of view, promoting its ideas and values. The American Revolution, among other things, was the beginning of shaking that dogma. This was followed 150 years later, at the outset of World War I, with an abrupt shift of global power from Europe to the United States. Eventually, Europe was forced to give up its colonies (though it never mentally de-colonized) and reluctantly acquiesced to a world in which its economic and military survival depended on the United States. It is too soon for Europe to accept this.

Indeed, the 2023–2024 assault on Judaism is occurring at a time that is:

- less than eighty years after the Zionist revolution and the emancipation of Jews from European oppression, as discussed above.

- about one hundred years after Europe's fall from grace, and the abrupt shift of power to the United States.

- only 250 years after the American Revolution and the emancipation of Americans from European dogmas.

Such seismic shifts take time to settle.

The United States was founded on an ideological bedrock of Americanism: freedom, particularity, nationalism, and faith. Europe, on the other hand, has pivoted over the last decades to values of universalism, counter-particularity, post-nationalism, and secularism.

America is rooted in Judeo-Christian values. Today's Europe is increasingly pivoting toward anti-theism, being a byproduct of the French Revolution. (The French attempt to change the week from seven to ten days just to refute the idea that God created the world was just one anti-theism tactic.)

The American Revolution was not just about the physical exodus from Europe to America. It was also an ideological exodus from Europe and the negation of centuries-old European frameworks. In one demonstration of today's contrast between Europeanism and Americanism, French President Macron stated in President Trump's presence in 2018: "Nationalism is a betrayal of patriotism." Yet nationalism is at the core of the American Revolution.

The American Revolution has been romanticized as a return to Zion. As a result, many towns and main streets in the United States were given Zionist names such as New Canaan, New Jerusalem, Mount Moriah, Bethel, and Shiloh.

Americanism is a form of abstract Zionism. The establishment of New Zion (America) is synergistic with the Jews' return to Old Zion (Israel). Both were conducted as an exodus from Europe. James Madison, one of America's founding fathers and its fourth president, learned Hebrew. The Founding Fathers even considered using Hebrew instead of English as the unifying language of the United States. As Christians reestablished a new Zion in a new land, Jews began the process of reestablishing Old Zion in their old land. Theodor Herzl said that "Zionism is the return to Judaism." In a similar manner, Americanism is the return to Christianity.

That Judeo-Christian journey toward return is 180 degrees opposite to the journey in Europe that occurred at the same time: Europe journeyed from faith to secularism to atheism, and increasingly to zealous anti-theism. As a result, Americanism became a primary Western ideology that preserves monotheistic

Christianity. Many viewed the attack on Judaism that followed October 7th as an attack on the Divine. If that is the case, then it is also an attack on Americanism, since both Israel and America are today's flag-carriers of monotheism.

Second Act of the American Revolution—the Ideological Phase

European powers have long ceded control of their colonies. The United Kingdom has not only accepted its "loss" of America but has formed the "special relationship" with the United States, a cornerstone of both nations' geopolitical doctrine.

But Europe is far from doing that and has been engaging in a low-octane resistance to the values of the American Revolution. Indeed, the European narrative is still very strong in America and growing. Some Americans welcome the prospect of the Europeanization of the American ideal, while others feel it negates the principles of the American Revolution. This is part of the legitimate debate in democracies.

Just as in the 18th century, the debate today is also about internal political disagreements in both the U.S. and Europe. There are "neo-Loyalists"/"neo-Tories" in the United States who promote European values in America, as there are those Europeans who promote American values in Europe. This is part of a democracy. Yet, it is important to emphasize that Europe is actively trying to Europeanize America, and the assault on Judaism plays a pivotal role in this attempt. If Americans welcome the erosion of the values of the American Revolution, then the national security aspects of the assault on Judaism are mostly on the practical levels discussed above. For example, they trigger the potential arrest of U.S. soldiers and government officials. But if Americans wish to defend the values of the American

Revolution, then the assault on Judaism represents an even greater threat to the essence of Americanism.

Indeed, just as Europe never fully accepted the American Revolution, it certainly never accepted the Zionist revolution, which only escalated the 2,300-year-old European opposition to Judaism.

<u>Europe vs. Israel</u>

As discussed, the Europe-Israel feud is the world's oldest conflict. While it had long periods of peace or containment (at times lasting for centuries), the Europe-Israel relationship has repeatedly cycled back to conflict following such periods.

The feud dates back to the Greek, and then Roman invasions of Judea. While other nations accepted the European invaders, the Jews rebelled. Centuries later, as a byproduct of those conquests, Europeans astonishingly accepted the Jews' monotheistic religion in the form of Christianity. This, one would think, should end the Europe-Israel feud, but it was just redirected to accommodate evolving European and Israeli realities.

Europe highjacked Christianity and drafted it into its persecution of Jews. As Europeans became Christians, they began slandering Jews through religious currencies. For example, the European attempt to eradicate Judaism in the 12th century was carried out in the name of religion (through the Crusades) as was a similar attempt in the 15th century (through the Inquisition). As discussed, when Europe all but abandoned religious Christianity, it redirected its opposition to Judaism through a new secular ideology developed in the 19th century: antisemitism.

It is naive to believe that the establishment of the Jewish state ended European opposition to Judaism. While both America and Israel came about through a process of transformation, Europe did not transform. Europe stayed Europe. Although Europe did not initiate the 2023–2024 assault on Judaism, it is part and parcel of it, as discussed in previous chapters. This participation is natural, given both the European-Israeli feud and the Europeanism-Americanism philosophical divide.

COUNTERING THE THREAT TO AMERICA

Judaism is under assault and the destruction mechanisms have been activated. This was true in the 1940s and is true in the 2020s.

In the 1940s, President Franklin D. Roosevelt evaluated the proposal to disrupt the destruction mechanisms of Judaism in the context of the range of threats the United States was facing at the time. He decided that intercepting the destruction mechanism of Judaism was not the priority. For the United States, neutralizing the death camps where the Nazis carried out their plan to eradicate Judaism by killing Jew-by-Jew, would have taken resources from other operations. This was a multi-arena world war, and a prioritization decision needed to be made. To say it coldly, FDR determined that disrupting the destruction mechanisms of Judaism would have taken away from defending America in other arenas.

In our era's assault on Judaism, it is the reverse: Disrupting the destruction mechanisms of Judaism is defending America. As discussed, the assault on Judaism embodies both a short-term and a long-term threat to America. Unlike in the 1940s, the United States today has the capability, capacity, and pressing national interest to disrupt the assault on Judaism on its multiple levels, using various tools at its disposal.

Sanctions

An obvious tool is sanctions against those who are committing the assault on Judaism—especially those who put U.S. interests and values in danger, such as the ICC.

Two precedents support imposing such sanctions: One is the sanctions President Trump imposed in 2020 on the ICC when it sought to investigate the United States. The other is the sanction regime that President Biden imposed in 2024 against Israeli Jews.

The same tenacity with which the Biden administration went after Israeli Jews can be deployed to go against those attacking Judaism—whether they are in the ICC, ICJ, the UN Human Rights Council, or elsewhere. Similarly, the U.S. can choose to impose sanctions on individuals, organizations, or countries that openly state that they are planning actions against the United States. The South African government stated openly that there are "150 lawyers" working on bringing suits against Israeli soldiers participating in the Gaza war, and that the U.S. is next.

Had South Africa known that there was a price to pay, it might have been deterred from partaking in the assault on Judaism, and through it, the assault on America. Similarly, had those 150 lawyers known that there was a price to pay, they might have been deterred from partaking in the assault on Judaism, and through it, the assault on America.

Sanctions is a powerful tool available for the United States, but it needs to be directed towards the threat America faces—one of which being the assault on Judaism.

A Matter of National Security, Not of Antisemitism

As discussed, the assault on Judaism is a national security threat to the United States. Therefore, the response needs to be on the national security level. The response should not be the appointment of more "Antisemitism czars" or planting trees in Israel. Indeed, the response should not be housed in a Jewish packaging but at the National Security Council.

The assault on Judaism is of course related to antisemitism, but having it managed by an "antisemitism envoy" is akin to having Israeli wines still being displayed in American wine stores in the "Kosher" section. Yes, they happen to be kosher, but that is not the point—they are top-rated wines winning medal after medal. Similarly, an incoming Category 5 hurricane is of course a matter of weather science, but no governor would appoint a science professor to manage his state's preparations and actions for that looming threat.

The assault on Judaism is no longer a "Jewish issue"; it is an American national security issue, and should be handled as such, including when it comes to dealing with U.S. allies.

A Foreign Policy Priority

On February 24, 2001, just a month after taking office, the Biden administration announced that it was "putting Human Rights at the center of U.S. foreign policy." The same should be done with the assault on Judaism.

The U.S. has ample leverage on those countries that participate in the assault, whether those countries are housing and funding the ICC and other institutions that assault Judaism; whether they are unilaterally recognizing the State of Palestine; whether they are supporting organizations that incite against Jews, or partaking in such incitement directly.

Turning the assault on Judaism into a foreign policy priority would lead to the incorporation of this issue into the ongoing bilateral dialogue that the United States has with its allies. The effect is not just in reactionary "punitive" measures after an assault is made by those countries, but also when it comes to deterrence. Would France announce that it would arrest Prime Minster Netanyahu upon orders of the ICC if it knew that such an announcement would be met by a U.S. response?

When France announced that it would arrest Netanyahu, it did not only threaten Israel but also the United States. France has set a dangerous precedent. If the ICC issues a surprise arrest warrant for a current or former U.S. president visiting France, presumably France would now be compelled to arrest him. Moreover, France's collaboration pledge could encourage the ICC to issue such an arrest warrant specifically when a U.S. president is visiting.

As it happened, President Biden visited France just a few weeks after France promised to comply with the ICC arrest warrants. Ironically, the state visit marked the 80th anniversary of the Normandy invasion. At the same time that American troops invaded Normandy to liberate Europe, the French government was collaborating with Germany, executing arrest warrants issued by the Germans against Jews.

Over twenty-nine thousand brave American troops died in Normandy in their battle to protect France, and over seventy thousand French Jews were arrested and then deported to their death—much thanks to the collaboration of the French government and their compliance with such arrest warrants. Unlike Germany, the French did not repent. In December 2020, President Macron announced his plans to honor Philippe Pétain, the head of the collaborative Vichy government, for his role in World War I. His role in the arrest of Jews during the previous attempt to eradicate Judaism was apparently not sufficiently relevant.

Biden stated in a June 8, 2024 press conference with President Macron: "France was our first friend and remains one of our best friends." Therefore, it is even more incumbent upon the United States to address France's collaboration with the ICC. It should be front and center in the bilateral discussions between the two countries. This can only happen if the assault on Judaism is treated by the United States as a national security threat and dealt with as a foreign policy priority. If it is not, then it will be easy to downplay the ICC warrant as merely an issue involving Israel and the Jews, and then deal with it through an antisemitism czar or a "committee against Israel-bashing."

The same goes for inciting statements of foreign leaders. When Canada's Trudeau incites the world against the Jews by accusing the Jewish state of indiscriminately killing women, children, and babies, the U.S. should consider summoning the Canadian ambassador for admonishment, which in turn could deter other leaders from using such inciting rhetoric. The signaling effect of this is just as important, as it sends a clear message regarding America's posture when it comes to the assault on Judaism.

End the Ludicrous Stance of Zero-Tolerance to Last Century's Threat

In 2021, President Biden appointed a commission to craft a national strategy to combat antisemitism, drawing on the leadership of Vice President Kamala Harris's husband Douglas Emhoff. The commission did something that is perhaps too common in making policy decisions: focus on the threat of the previous era, while ignoring the threat of today.

Traditional antisemitism is indeed a threat to the safety of Jews, but not to the survival of Judaism. As discussed, Israel-bashing, on the other hand, is both a larger threat to the safety of Jews (estimated to account for as much as 70 percent of anti-Jewish attacks in America, even before October 7th), and an existential threat to Judaism, since unlike traditional antisemitism, Israel-bashing triggers the destruction mechanisms of Judaism. Yet the focus remained on fighting last century's battle.

It is time to end the prevailing absurdity of expressing zero tolerance for traditional antisemitism, the existential threat to Judaism in the 20th century, while giving a green light for Israel-bashing, the existential threat to Judaism in the 21st century. This can get an official government stamp of approval through a new commission that would tailor the national strategy to the threat.

Ending this outdated posture would also allow the United States to counter the threat in various domestic arenas. For example, universities depend on the U.S. government on multiple levels: for tax-exempt status, funding, permits, and partnerships. Universities cannot survive without the support of the government. American universities played a pivotal role in the assault on Judaism, even before October 7th, but certainly in the days that followed the Hamas attack. By May 2024, the U.S. academic infrastructure was disrupted due to the activities of Israel-bashers/pro-Palestinian protesters. There can be a debate as to what point the U.S. government should intervene, but certain activities should trigger intervention, under the new proposed guidelines of "zero-tolerance to Israel-bashing." When universities encourage demonstrations supporting Hamas's October 7th atrocities, it is time to intervene. When university presidents refuse to condemn calls for the genocide of Jews due to Israel-bashing, it is time to intervene. When they give a green light to anti-Jewish incitement due to Israel-bashing, it is time to intervene.

Congresswoman Elise Stefanik scolded university presidents for those actions during a December 2023 congressional hearing.

This was met with great gratitude in Israel. As Israelis were on the frontlines defending from the physical assault on Judaism, Stefanik was on the frontline of defending from the ideological assault on Judaism.

The giant poster in Jerusalem with the photo of President Biden with the words "Thank you" that was placed in October near the residence of the U.S. ambassador to Israel was replaced with a new giant poster—this one with a photo of Stefanik with the words "You are great!"

Disassociate the Assault on Judaism from the Palestinian Issue

As discussed, the aftermath of October 7th, made it clear: The ideological assault on Judaism from the West is not a byproduct of the Israel-Palestinian conflict. To some extent, it is the reverse.

It is time to correct a lingering falsehood from the 1970s still prevalent in U.S. foreign policy circles—that if we solve the Israeli-Arab conflict, Jews and Judaism would be safe, and so would be the rest of the world.

As discussed, age-old opposition to Judaism is rooted in the 2,300-year-old European-Israeli feud, not in the Palestinian issue. For example, the reason Europe was so adamantly opposed to the United States moving its embassy to Jerusalem was its steadfast position that no part of Jerusalem should belong to Israel. Yet, the European position is that no part of Jerusalem should belong to the Palestinians either; instead, it should belong to the "international community" (a laundered term for Europe).

Getting rid of that 1970s falsehood would reduce the pressure the U.S. government is under to have some sort of solution "now" to the Palestinian issue no matter the consequences ("Ceasefire Now," "Peace Now," "Two-State Solution Now"). It would pave the way for the U.S. to focus its efforts on long-term strategic frameworks that are organic to the region, such as the Abraham Accords, as opposed to glib and slogan-based frameworks that are imposed on the region by the West. An example of that was seen in the fall of 2020, in a virtual "split screen." On one side of the screen, Israelis were flocking to Dubai, forging business partnerships with Arabs, establishing new regional businesses, and forming strong friendships.

On the other side, European diplomats were flocking to a hill in southern Jerusalem to protest the construction of a new neighborhood that would house both Arabs and Jews, since that neighborhood is situated beyond the "Green Line" and hence sabotaged the idea of a two-state solution—which of course is needed "now" to prevent global instability and eventually lead to peace and cooperation between Israelis and Arabs (which was actually happening live on the other side of the screen).

On one side of the screen, faith-based Abrahamic nations were forging partnerships under American leadership, choosing essence (actual regional integration) over slogans. On the other side, Europeans were sabotaging peaceful coexistence between Israelis and Arabs, choosing slogans ("two-state solution!") over essence.

<u>End the Irrational Obsession with the Two-State Solution</u>

While the idea of the two-state solution was rejected by both Israelis and Arabs, it has been considered sacrosanct in Western policy circles. I recall attending a book talk at the American Colony Hotel in East Jerusalem in 2016, alongside officials from the UN, EU, and NGOs, and some Palestinian intellectuals. At the champagne reception that preceded the talk, one senior

European diplomat warned me: "We are about to witness political blasphemy."

The book by international peacemaker Padraig O'Malley was titled *The Two-State Delusion*, and as the title suggested, strongly rejected that idea. In the Q&A that followed, the Palestinians in the audience belittled the author's thesis, saying that he was stating the obvious. Palestine is one state, and of course, the two-state solution is a Western delusion that has nothing to do with them. On the other hand, the Westerners in the room had a very different reaction, which was angry and combative: "What about us?" they scolded the author, "We invested years of our career in developing this template."

Recalling Herzl's observation that politicians' obsession with being consistent prevents them from doing the right thing for their country, it is indeed hard to let go of a slogan.

When a friend of mine ran for Congress in a Democratic primary, she met me ahead of her interview with Democratic Party bosses, who could open the doors to the party's donor base. Putting aside political views, she is a highly competent patriotic American who was leaving a successful business career in order to serve her country. "What should I say when they ask me about the Israeli-Palestinian conflict?" she asked me. "One line," I answered. "The Two-State solution." What does it entail? They don't know themselves. It is a slogan, a right-of-passage, a prerequisite to getting funding for your campaign.

Since then, one of the legends of the American Foreign Policy establishment, Henry Kissinger, joined the "political blasphemy" and turned against the two-state solution. In one of his final interviews before his death, published in *Politico* on December 12, 2023, he advised dropping the two-state solution, stating, "It is no longer viable."

The Gaza war subsequently delivered the two-state solution its final blow, not with the physical assault by Hamas, but with the ideological assault that followed from the West. The two-state solution was based on the establishment of a demilitarized Palestinian state with various restrictions to accommodate Israel's security needs, such as Israel controlling the Palestinian state's airspace and border crossings.

The West—including the UN, the media, and Western politicians—placed Hamas's October 7th attacks in the context of the occupation of Gaza. If Gaza was under occupation, when there was not a single Israeli soldier or settler, then certainly the future state of Palestine would be under occupation: There would be an Israeli military presence, settlement blocks, and ample restrictions. Hence, global public opinion would utterly reject the idea of an "occupied" state of Palestine, which is the cornerstone of the two-state solution.

All that a two-state solution would do is switch some of the banners of the assault on Judaism, though some banners would stay, such as "From the river to the sea." At least now, the thinking goes, two states could negotiate this dispute on equal terms. (Oh, and no worries—if terrorism came out of the state of Palestine, the Jewish state would have the "moral high ground," and the world would be behind it when it retaliated, just as it promised it would be behind it after the 2005 withdrawal from Gaza.)

October 7th happened, to some extent, because of such linkage. The logic in 2005 was that sooner or later there would be a two-state solution that would lead to an era of safety for Jews as well as to global acceptance of Judaism and the Jewish state. While there will be negotiations over borders, settlements, and various other aspects, it is clear that in any final agreement, Gaza would not be part of the Jewish state, but part of the Palestinian state. Therefore, since the two-state solution will inevitably happen sooner or later, Israel might as well withdraw now from Gaza.

Israel withdrew in 2005, Hamas took over in 2007, and after years of military build-up, attacked on October 7, 2023. Hamas's physical assault fueled the large-scale ideological assault on Judaism from the West, which by 2024 has turned into an existential threat to Judaism as well as a strategic threat to America.

INTERCEPTING THE PATH TO ERADICATE JUDAISM

When doing a threat assessment, one needs to study both the intention and the capabilities of the attacker posing the threat. Israel failed twice by over-focusing on the intention.

In its 1973 failure, the assessment was that Egypt did not intend to attack since it knew it could not win. Israel failed to recognize that the Egyptian objective was not victory in war, but restoration of the Arab honor lost in 1967 when it suffered a humiliating defeat. Temporary victory sufficed. The lesson of the 1973 war was to focus the threat assessment on the attacker's capabilities, not only rely on psychoanalysis of its intentions.

In the October 7, 2023 failure, the conception again was that Hamas did not intend to attack since it was deterred. Israel failed to recognize that Hamas was set to acquire counter-deterrence assets in the hostages it took, the civilian population, and mostly the Western media, which would create public pressure that would handicap Israel's abilities to carry on the war and destroy Hamas. A likely early lesson of the October 7th failure is, indeed, that one needs to focus the threat assessment on the capabilities of Hamas, and not only on whether they are likely to follow through or not.

Today, as the Jewish nation is facing the greatest threat to its survival in two thousand years—a threat that is coming from the West, it is imperative to apply the lessons of 1973 and 2023 and not rely on the intentions of allies, but rather focus on the capabilities. Those capabilities, as discussed in the book, are already deployed, and the assault on Judaism is already in its advanced stages.

Hard-core Israel-bashers fueled the assault, and Israel-basher-lites activated the destruction mechanisms. Yet Israel-bashers can only go so far down the path to eradicate Judaism. They need to engage the full power of governments. As it became clear in 2024 that European and other governments opted to participate in the contemporary assault on Judaism, it is now left up to the United States to use its leverage to intercept the path to the destruction of Judaism, and in doing so protect America from a growing threat to its national security.

A FREE ISRAEL WOULD ADVANCE HUMANITY

Judaism is under an existential threat. The Jewish motto turned song, "In every generation, someone rises up to eradicate us" became more relevant than ever in 2024.

Yet Jews in Israel know one thing for certain: One way or another, we will survive. The question Queen Esther faced was not if Judaism would persevere through that generation's attempt to eradicate it, but whether she would be the one to save Judaism. As she was told by her uncle Mordechai: If you stay silent at this time, "then relief and deliverance will arise for the Jews from another place."

Nations around the world today face a similar choice: They can join the assault on Judaism, as many of them have done through 2024—whether through slandering the Jewish nation or through announcing their intention to collaborate with arrest warrants for Jews—or they can join the battle to save Judaism. The choice cannot be clearer: to be among those who bless, or to be among those who curse.

Jews in Israel and elsewhere need to be aware that the assault on Judaism is here to stay for a long time. It is arrogant to think otherwise. For 2,300 years, Europe has opposed Judaism. It is less than eighty years since Jews and Judaism returned to their land, and merely fifty years since they returned to Jerusalem. Processes like this take time. Herzl warned the father of German nationalism and Germany's first chancellor, Otto von Bismarck, about the fallacy of just "canceling" antisemitism: "There is no use in suddenly announcing in the newspaper that starting tomorrow, all people are equal." The assault on Judaism is rooted in deep dogmatic thinking and as discussed, it is intertwined with the growing philosophical chasm of our time, Europeanism versus Americanism.

While Herzl understood that European opposition to Judaism is chronic, he also believed that once a Jewish state was established, Jews would be transformed from being the "sea lion" defined by the ocean of European persecution to being a real lion who is free and strong. At that point, those free and strong Jews in the Jewish state would advance humanity in unimaginable ways. The Jewish state will exist because it will be the necessity of the world, as Herzl concluded: "The world will be liberated by our freedom, enriched by our wealth, and magnified by our greatness."

In 2024, the Jewish state is not yet fully free. The assault on Judaism through Israel-bashing robs the world of the full potential for advancements that could be made by the Jewish state. Israelis are concerned about arrest warrants, sanctions, asset confiscations, and incitement in the Western media. And this is on top of being forced to defend themselves from the physical assault by Hamas, Iran, and its proxies.

"The eternal nation is not afraid of a long road," reads another popular Jewish motto turned into a song. The road ahead is indeed long. The assault on Judaism will only intensify in the coming years. Still, in the meantime, Jews in Israel remain grateful for living in a country that Herzl called "a new and happy form of human society," and in doing so, being a beacon to humanity.

The conversation continues on:
TheAssaultOnJudaism.com

Please visit the book's website for endnotes, a list of referenced
books, articles, and songs, as well as updates on upcoming
events and additional resources.

For media and book-tour inquiries:
media@TheAssaultOnJudaism.com

ACKNOWLEDGMENTS

I would like to thank the brave men and women of the IDF—the wondrous generation that rose up to defend the Jewish nation and Western civilization. No sanctions, demoralization efforts, or slanderous war crime indictments would deter them and our nation. With God's help, we will prevail—both in the physical assault and the ideological assaults on Judaism.

I would also like to thank the members of the US Armed Forces, who provide a security umbrella to the world. I am fortunate to be born into an era when, after two thousand years, I can live at home, in sovereignty, amongst my people—a miracle I am constantly grateful for. I want to thank my family, in particular, my wife Tamar, a beacon of faith, who in a year when I lost both my mother and grandmother was there to represent the promise of a brighter future.

I want to thank Post Hill Press, especially Madeline Sturgeon and Anthony Ziccardi, for bringing this book to life so expeditiously, as well as to those who read drafts on short notice, including David Brummer, Ruth Krieger, and Bennett Ruda. Also, to members of the Judaism 3.0 think tank, readers of my previous book *Judaism 3.0*, and my *Jerusalem Post* column— many of whom send reactions that are helpful in fine-tuning my thinking.

Finally, to you, the readers. I hope this book provides the motivation to partake in the defense of Judaism. And for that, I send my gratitude and blessings from Jerusalem.

Gol Kalev is a columnist at *The Jerusalem Post* who analyzes long-term global geopolitical shifts, European developments, and trends in Zionism, Judaism, and Israel. His analysis articles have also appeared in *The Jerusalem Report*, *Israel Hayom*, *The Daily Wire*, *The Media Line*, *The Washington Times*, *Newsweek*, and *Foreign Policy*.

He is the author of *Judaism 3.0: Judaism's Transformation to Zionism* and chairman of the Judaism 3.0 think tank (formally the America-Israel Friendship League think tank). He is also a Herzl scholar and has written numerous articles applying the thinking of the Jewish state's visionary to today's strategic issues.

Growing up in Tel Aviv and serving in the Israeli army, he then lived in New York where he was an investment banker, specializing in mergers and acquisitions and capital raising for financial institutions globally. He also spent time in various European cities and has traveled through both the American and European countryside, learning about contrasting world-views. He now lives in Jerusalem.